As words become exclusively emotional

they cease to be words

and therefore of course

cease to perform

any strictly linguistic function.

They operate as growls or barks or tears. . . .

They die as words

not because there is too much emotion in them

but because there is too little—

and finally nothing at all—

of anything else.

*C. S. LEWIS, STUDIES IN WORDS*


Let the word of Christ dwell in you richly . . .

*COLOSSIANS 3:16*

# GOD Talk

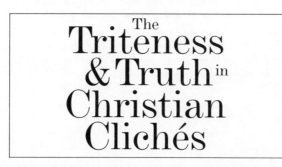

The
Triteness
& Truth in
Christian
Clichés

Randall J. VanderMey

INTERVARSITY PRESS
DOWNERS GROVE, ILLINOIS 60515

InterVarsity Press® is the book-publishing division of InterVarsity Christian Fellowship®, a student movement active on campus at hundreds of universities, colleges and schools of nursing in the United States of America, and a member movement of the International Fellowship of Evangelical Students. For information about local and regional activities, write Public Relations Dept., InterVarsity Christian Fellowship, 6400 Schroeder Rd., P.O. Box 7895, Madison, WI 53707-7895.

ISBN 0-8308-1348-9

Printed in the United States of America ∞

**Library of Congress Cataloging-in-Publication Data**

VanderMey, Randall.
    God talk: the triteness and truth in Christian clichés/Randall
 J. VanderMey.
      p.    cm.
    ISBN 0-8308-1348-9
    1. Language and languages—Religious aspects—Christianity.
  2. Christianity—Terminology.  I. Title.
  BR115.L25V36  1993
  230'.014—dc20                93-18087
                                     CIP

| 17 | 16 | 15 | 14 | 13 | 12 | 11 | 10 | 9 | 8 | 7 | 6 | 5 | 4 | 3 | 2 | 1 |
|----|----|----|----|----|----|----|----|----|----|----|----|----|----|----|----|----|
| 06 | 05 | 04 | 03 | 02 | 01 | 00 | 99 | 98 | 97 | 96 | 95 | 94 | 93 | | | |

# Acknowledgments

Among the many who helped to nurse this book along I must acknowledge Helen Bonzelaar, for her early enthusiasm; Sandra VanderMey, for her patient listening and unerring advice; Sheridan Blau and the South Coast Writing Project (SCWriP) at UCSB, for proving that evangelical Christians aren't the only ones who "share"; Eugene and Helen Westra, for listening with the inner ear; Greg Spencer, Paul Willis, Kathy McClymond and Steve Cook, for conscientious and creative repartee; Gerald Bouma, for boosting my thoughts about entertainment and worship; Mark-Philip Venema, for laughing in all the right places; Homer and Joanne VanderMey, for enduring much and appreciating more; many students at Westmont College, and particularly Cassie Londo, for giving me an image of my audience; Jonathan Wilson, for his remarks on "spiritual warfare"; Marianne Walker, for lending her grace to the mechanics of production; and Rodney Clapp, whose generosity of spirit and tactfulness in criticism should be the envy of every editor and the hope of every writer.

# Introduction: Inwards and In-Words

It is more dangerous to tread on the corns of a live giant than to cut off the head of a dead one: but it is more useful and better fun.

C. S. LEWIS, *STUDIES IN WORDS*

*I* suppose this book began when I was a child, growing up in Grand Rapids, Michigan, among second- and third-generation Dutch immigrants, more or less staunch Calvinists all. In my Christian home, at my Christian school, at my Christian Reformed church, in the Christian marketplace and at the Christian beaches (yes, there are such things), I heard stock phrases—in-words—that both fascinated and disturbed me. I'm not referring to phrases repeated rhythmically and with ritual power in Christian liturgy but to phrases that trip off the tongue—and trip up the mind—in everyday conversation.

"Fold your hands and close your eyes," said my parents before our modest, well-ordered meals. Before my voyages into the dream-kingdom I was taught to pray, "Now I lay me down to sleep, I pray thee, Lord, my soul to keep . . ." Our bodies, when there was danger of our defiling them, were called "God's temples." New babies were "gifts from God." Some marriages were "made in heaven." People shared "joys and concerns" in church, where a bad duet was called "special music." The senior man at a public banquet would "say grace." Letters were signed "Yours in Christ." God "wanted us to succeed" and "never sent us burdens greater than we could bear." If someone died, it was "God's will" and the deceased was "in a better place." Any event, even a funeral—especially a funeral—was a time to "praise the Lord."

Writing and literature, as they became my love and profession, took me from the Midwest to the eastern urban corridor, back to the Midwest for a long sojourn and, most recently, to dry, roiling Southern California. As I moved, I encountered different communities of Christians and, on their lips, new phrases. They prayed for "traveling mercies." They were "prayer warriors" who waged "spiritual warfare." They had "burdens" for the "unchurched," received "words of knowledge," had "a heart for missions." This "world was not their home." They were "in it but not of it." They "walked their talk" and would "pray for you" in their "quiet time."

Before I could turn my fascination and uneasiness with such language into a book, however, several things had to happen. First, I had to become conscious of my subject. All my life I must have been half-consciously flinching at the sound of Christian clichés, because to the best of my ability I had barred them from my vocabulary. But when I stopped at last to count them, I was amazed. Forty, sixty, a hundred and ten, and eventually over a hundred and seventy phrases packed my list, and more kept arriving as friends and students offered their insights. I began to read newspapers, magazines and books with tuned ear and open eye. I made Christian language a subject of conversation. And yet I'm sure I have gathered only a small sampling of the phrases in use.

Next, I had to acknowledge my own discomfort. That might not appear hard to do after a lifetime of maintaining ironic distance between myself and the language of my tribe. But it was. The *reason* I had maintained a distance (apart from some youthful cynicism, which I regret) was to keep from stumbling over what I thought were linguistic corpses as I struggled to grow into a living relationship with language, with people and with God. Focusing on dead and dying language had seemed like majoring in minors, so to speak, while missing the genuine spiritual dramas in people's lives.

My reluctance dissolved after I began to reflect that the habit of using stock phrases can sometimes be not only a symptom but also a cause of spiritual paralysis. It signals a dulling of vision, and such dulling is in no one's best interest. As George Orwell argued almost fifty years ago, a loss of sensitivity to logic and nuance in language makes us lose touch with wellsprings of power as well as processes of change, in ourselves and in our world. Having thus become ossified, massified and pacified, we are more readily subject to the rule of tyrants.

In the religious world, Orwell's prophecy is most obviously fulfilled in the case of the cults, which are notorious for manipulating language to sedate their victims and forge them into a politically wieldy mass. But one need not be an extremist, nor need one be religious, to feel the allure of the anesthetized life, particularly in this age of Walkmans, couch potatoes, television jingles and Muzak. I have felt the allure as much as the next person, and so I felt entitled to speak of it.

Next, however, I had to gather courage to speak about language despite my awareness of how bewilderingly vast a field it is. There was etymology to consider, semantics, stylistics, rhetoric, speech act theory, psycholinguistics, semiotics, sociolinguistics, cultural anthropology and more. There were Nietzsche, Barfield, Hayakawa and others, from Wittgenstein to Vygotsky, looking down from their respective eminences. In such company, the only way I could presume to offer my insights was to decide that I had come to this task not only to teach about language but also—and far more—to learn. I decided simply to haul out the raw material, talk about the subject for which my life had been a long tutorial, and enjoy my time exploring it. In that way I found the courage to clamber up onto the living giant, language, and tap-dance on its corns.

But even then I was not ready. I soon discovered that merely disapproving of stock phrases brought me no enjoyment. Negativism does not edify. Nor could I pretend that my own language was exempt from clichés. In short, I found it harder to maintain a positive attitude than I had expected, and I soon reached a spiritual crisis.

After a few early trials, I discovered that there was no way to write the book except to pledge that I would grow in it spiritually as well as intellectually. To pledge that as I spoke of dead ends, I would venture down open roads. That as I spoke of spiritual barrens, I would seek spiritual plenty such as I had never known before— awakenings, humblings, flowerings, reversals. Unless each piece would bring me news from the spiritual frontiers, I was determined to throw it away.

At last, when the writing became a search rather than a synopsis, it began to repay me with energy, new direction, surprise and delight. It grew up intertwined with reading, prayer and new relationships.

From the start I had determined not to write a glossary of all the phrases I knew but to choose a few that moved me most and to write a short essay about each. I wanted to consider each thoughtless phrase and think the unthought. I wanted to understand not only what was meant by each phrase but also what was *done* with it and what *could* be meant in its place. In that way, I hoped to create a thought-formation that would attach itself to each phrase and forever change its timbre in my mind and in the minds of my readers.

Finally, it occurred to me that stock phrases tend to appear at the critical junctures of our lives. They grease the hinges. At times when we confront our deeper hopes and fears—times of transition, times of confrontation, times of triumph, times of horror, times of meeting and parting—we call up our own community's collective mastery of experience, its popular wisdom, in the form of what I would call "chronic" language. Such language—stock phrases, bromides, clichés, truisms, lingo, jargon—allows us to acknowledge the experience of life's open moments without having to experience the raw pain or joy of it ourselves. It eases us through various contexts for communication, without our tripping over our tongues or ignoring our circumstances, granted, but also without our having to invent.

Think of chronic language as something like speech but closer to ventriloquism, where our society throws the voice and we are the dummies. At best, it is sweet piety in humble uniform. Most of the time, it is a kind of uninspired and uninspiring ceremony, little more than a ritual checking of perimeters for the in-group. At worst, it is pseudopiety and a venal form of empty rhetoric.

I decided at the outset to let the order of my essays trace the generic pattern of a Christian life, a long arc from conception to the afterlife, segmented by those critical junctures to which I referred above: births, bedtimes, private talks about the "facts of life," mealtimes, church services, weddings, road trips, successes, disasters, illnesses, funerals and the times of our lives in between. What emerges from that outline is a strange macrolife, a slowly and heavily stirring giant that corresponds to the giant of language. Look within it and you will see not one but many lives, and many scenes from life, scenes I've lived, as in "Good Thoughts," scenes I've observed, as in "God Told Me," and scenes that are true enough to have happened, even if they didn't, as in "God Never Sends Us Burdens Greater Than We Can Bear."

What I learned in the course of writing, better than I knew before, was that human life extends not only *along* such arcs but *inward* as well, at every point. The mysteries of life's origins and ends attend every moment in the midst of life. We have only to open our minds to them to experience their depth.

In one's desire for such experience, however, language is not exclusively an ally. Speaking is an action, a physical participation in the movement of life; but at the same time, it is a diversion of mental energy into the thickets of linguistic symbol and system. Words point to the world, but they point, as well, to other words. Thus, speech gives us something but costs something, too. It both reveals and conceals. In speech it is hard to make the mind available to the mysteries of life. As soon as language becomes opaque, as it does when we resort to tried-and-true phrases, the mysteries close.

Here and there I have struck the note of satire. Elsewhere I have blamed or bemoaned. My overall purpose, however, is not to make anyone's speech sound bad or to make my own sound better. My primary interest, in fact, is not even in language, except as speech turns out to be, along with behavior and thought, the site of spiritual conflict. What looks from one side like treading on a giant's corns appears from the other side like wrestling with an angel or a devil. For as Christian language walks on stilts or harbors fear or signals the aimlessness of a herd, it accompanies the closing of the Christian mind. The good news is that close attention to Christian language—its possibilities as well as its poverties—can open the mind, reawaken wonder and strengthen faith.

# The Quick and the Dead

R omantic poets have beguiled us into thinking of the sublime as something grand, misty and remote. But according to the first great commentator on the subject, the ancient Greek author Longinus, sublime language is an excellence in expression which transports the listener. A sublime expression proceeds from a certain greatness of soul and employs a natural economy of words. It communicates "power and irresistible might," says Longinus, and gives our soul "joy and vaunting, as though it had itself produced what it has heard."

Whom does Longinus cite as an example of a speaker with sublime elevation of mind? Surprise: it's Moses. Among his many references to Homer he tucks in one little reference to "the legislator of the Jews," who is able to represent the divine nature as it really is, "pure and great and undefiled." The passage he cites as proof is from the first chapter of Genesis: "Let there be light, and there was light."

Longinus had a superb insight. Indeed, his sample passages from

Homer's *Odyssey* sound ornate and bombastic beside the power and might of the simple creation account in Genesis. Where power is greatest, there is least commotion.

But pardon my boldness if I propose an additional scriptural model of sublime speech. Mine focuses not on the beginning of the great pageant of history but on the end. I have in mind the seventh statement of the Apostles' Creed: "From thence he shall come to judge the quick and the dead." This line echoes Acts 10:42, in which Peter preaches to Cornelius about the spreading of the good news to the Gentiles as well as the Jews. "He commanded us . . . to testify," said Peter, "that it is he which was ordained of God to be the Judge of quick and dead" (KJV). Though the Apostles' Creed did not take its present form until about A.D. 650, the recurrence of this phrase, "the quick and the dead," in Romans 14:9, 2 Timothy 4:1 and 1 Peter 4:5 shows, according to some commentators, that simple, eloquent creedal formulations were already arising in the first century A.D.

If God's sowing of the seeds of creation is described with magisterial simplicity in Genesis 1, the language of Peter echoed in the Apostles' Creed is equally sublime in describing Christ's gathering of the harvest. What phrase could better convey the unchallenged authority in Christ's hand than the effortless phrase "to judge the quick and the dead"? In few words, it leaves out nothing.

Unfortunately, nothing in life as we know it is completely sublime. The only time you and I are likely to hear "the quick and the dead" it will probably sound like a flub. We will be standing in church reciting the Apostles' Creed. Probably 98 percent of us will use the contemporary wording, "the living and the dead." But a smattering of old-timers will cling to the King James English that constitutes for them the language of the true faith: "the quick and the dead." With "the quick" competing against "the living," the congregation will momentarily stutter like an ill-tuned engine. Children may wonder why such cacophony should arise during the reciting of a statement of unity.

Well, should it?

I can think of three replies. The first is a simple reflex: Nobody speaks of "the quick" anymore. Let archaic words die out, and let Christians speak contemporary language in unison.

However, I'm not quite that ready to let "the quick" die. I know of few English words with a better pedigree, and I'm still discovering the richness of what it means. By 1611, when "the quick and the dead" appeared in the King James version of the Bible, the phrase had already been in use for over seven hundred years, influenced by early translations of the Apostles' Creed and translations of the Bible from the Latin Vulgate. The Old English form *cwic* or *cwicu* supported a host of meanings implying live, alive, moving or sensitive. We still speak, relatedly, of biting a fingernail to the quick or of a baby's quickening in the womb. Used collectively, "the quick" means the living, those who manifest the spark of life, as opposed to corpses. And the word even has the virtue of sounding like what it means: it's quick.

The Indo-European root, *gwei*, that led to the Old English *cwic* developed by different routes into the Latin word *vivus* (from which come *vivid, vivacious, revive,* etc.) and the Greek words *bios* ("life," as in *biology*) and *zōon* ("a living being," as in *zoology* and *protozoa*). The latter is the very word that Peter used for "the quick" (or living) in Acts 10:42. So *cwic* is a distant cousin of *zōon*. That makes "the quick and the dead" an excellent translation.

I'm not quite so charmed, on the other hand, by the word-history of the word *living*. Its root, the Indo-European *leip,* means "stick to" or "adhere"; from that root we have also derived such appetizers as *liver* and *liposuction!* "The living" suggests literally those who stick together (unlike the dead, who fall apart).

If the word *cwic,* with all its directness and energy, all its mystery and power, has survived in the formal recitation of the Apostles' Creed for over a thousand years now, what compelling reason can there be for this generation to trade it in? My second reply, therefore, is the opposite of the first: Let the archaic word live, but let's relearn it.

My third reply is more fanciful. Listen appreciatively to the clash between *quick* and *living* as the old-timers have their say. Savor the difference. Feel the friction. Sense how linguistic traditions diverge, but how two differently textured meanings converge. Maybe when you feel the space between things, and yet the glue that binds them, and the spirit that moves them, you will know better what it means to be "quick." Maybe when you understand what kind of a creature will stand judgment at the end of time—a quick/living one—you will better understand the difference between a gamete and a zygote. Between a discardable scraping of placental tissue and a human embryo. Maybe you will have a better idea, then, why a metaphor works and how a man and a woman can love.

Maybe then, starting from a minor annoyance in church, you will better understand the sublime words of Genesis 2:7: "And the LORD God formed man of the dust of the ground, and breathed into his nostrils the breath of life; and man became a living soul" (KJV).

# A Gift
# from God

J ournal entry, June 4, 1991

Here it is, my thirty-ninth birthday. If ever I should be comfortable referring to a baby as a "gift from God," I suppose it should be today. It's hard to think of my own birth as anything other than a gift—I'm one-hundred percent sure I didn't earn it. And as I sit at my desk, scribbling, my young daughter, whose birth seems a gift to me beyond thanksgiving, says the day's first "Happy Birthday" and reminds me that my birth is a gift to her, too. If tradition holds, the same sentiment should be arriving from my parents in today's mail.

"A gift from God." Even the pope throws his weight behind the phrase. This morning's newspaper reports on the angry antiabortion sermon John Paul II preached in his native Poland, where abortion has been the principal form of birth control since 1956. He lashed out at the Polish parliament for postponing legislation that would have outlawed it.

"For the children to honor their parents," the pontiff preached in an impassioned commentary on the Fourth Commandment, "they must be considered and accepted as a gift from God. . . . Indeed, each and every child is a gift from God. That gift is always priceless, even if it is sometimes difficult to accept." An unborn child, said the pope, is never an intruder or aggressor. "He is a human being, and therefore he has the right to receive from his parents the unstinted gift of their own selves, even if that would require particular sacrifice on their part."

There. Straight from the most prominent leader in the Christian world: Each and every child is a gift from God.

Why, then, am I still uneasy with the phrase? Partly, I guess, because in common parlance *gift* brings to mind images of pretty wrappings and bows. But I was there, with camera, when our "gift" was given, and I saw the vernix and blood. The two images don't square. Oh, yes, *gift* is a figure of speech, and I can look past it. I do. But, even figuratively, to what does it refer? A baby doesn't magically appear on its birth day, like some present under a tinseled tree. We all know that. So when is the "gift" given? No literal hand forms the baby in the womb—we've seen the historic *Life* photo spreads of the developing fetus. We know about blastulas and zygotes, mitosis and meiosis, ovulation, ejaculation, intercourse, the gleam in the eye. All inquiry into the giving of the gift turns into a tracing of the life cycle, which goes spiraling back toward the horizon of human memory like coils of barbed wire, until it reaches the only fencepost in sight: Adam. "The LORD God . . . breathed into his nostrils the breath of life, and the man became a living being" (Gen 2:7). Now, there was a gift from God.

But when did *I* become a "gift from God"? Was I nothing more than an aspiring tumor until my first kick at the tummy wall rang the bell: "Special delivery"? Was I mysteriously, miraculously, divinely and individually ensouled somewhere near the end of my mother's second trimester, around the time when the legal franchise on abortion runs out? Did I twinkle into existence at the precise moment when the last polypeptide strand in the DNA from my maternal germ cell locked onto its paternal counterpart?

I believe such questions may be asked without irreverence to God, but the more I press them the murkier the answers become. At the end of my quiz, I am forced to confess, with Job, "Surely I spoke of things I did not understand, things too wonderful for me to know" (Job 42:3). If I wanted to know how God gives the gift of life, to adapt words from the Middle English author William Langland, my eyes ought to be in my arse.

But there is another way to understand the phrase "a gift from God," a way that preserves it from the biological myths and pious sentiments with which we tend to encumber it. The "gift" that new parents receive is not merely the eight pounds of joy in their arms. It is their fertility, which they share with their baby and the whole of their race. A baby, therefore, is not first of all a deposit in the parents' personal fund of happiness. To treat it as such is to make a big, materialistic mistake. A baby is to be given up, not hoarded. To think of a baby as personal enrichment—a precious gift—is to turn that child into a commodity, whereas to rejoice in the whole divine endowment of the human race—our collective gift *for* giving birth—is to affirm that child's full creaturehood, along with ours, along with the power of the Creator.

Lewis Hyde has pointed out, in *The Gift,* that not only the ancient Israelites but also many other societies all over the world have traditionally emphasized that gift-giving is a cycle. A gift loses its meaning as soon as it becomes property. Instead of pooling up in some hogpen of wealth, it must be given again. This is the paradox: "When the gift is used, it is not used up. Quite the opposite . . . : the gift that is not used will be lost, while the one that is passed along remains abundant."

"In the world of gift," says Hyde, "you not only have your cake and eat it too, you can't have your cake *unless* you eat it."

The great distinctiveness of the ancient Israelites was that their God was in the giving loop. Fruits, grains, cattle, babies—all came from God's mysterious hand. Through sacrifice of firstfruits, God's gifts were to be passed along, back into the great mystery of divine providence and on into the hands of his representatives, the priests and the poor, before they could be experienced as a blessing. Any other use of God's good gifts would call down a curse. Such was the secret of a Nazirite like Samson, whose unshorn locks symbolized a return of his life to Yahweh. And such was the prophetic wisdom in little Samuel's answer: "Here I am."

So here I am, everybody. Happy Birthday!

# Now I Lay Me Down to Sleep

aw a little window in my skull over the right temporal lobe. Plant a thin wire electrode in my cerebral cortex—carefully please! Now zap me with a couple milliamperes of electrical current. I'll stay awake during this delicate fishing expedition and tell you what afternoons, what songs, what dreams you've hooked. Ease to the right a few centimeters. A little deeper now, closer to the seats of fear and rage and love. All right, power up.

Wow. What are you doing?

I'm getting a picture of something I haven't seen for thirty-five years. It's dark. I'm in my Huckleberry Hound pajamas, just the bottoms. My underpants are so tight they chafe. The pajama legs bind my shins.

I had completely forgotten those Huckleberry Hound pajamas.

With my bare toes, I'm kneading the loops of a weary old circle rug. I guess I'm kneeling. This is so real to me. I feel cold droplets of water between my shoulder blades. My mom is stroking my burr haircut with her crusty hand. My head still feels warm and pulpy from the bath. I'm so clean. Wait. I'm saying something—

Now Ilay medown tosleep

Ipray theeLord mysoul tokeep

IfI shouldie before Iwake

Ipray theeLord mysoul totake.

Lorbless MommyanDaddy anJimmyanCarolanDanny

andallthatwelove, Amen.

I forgot I used to pray that. Now I'm jumping in bed and kicking off the sheets as my mom tries to cover me. She is saying "You little stinker" and kissing my forehead.

Power off. Stop. Stop.

I want to save this. I have no idea where that prayer has been hiding all these years. I can't tell you all the feelings it brings back. If I thought you would excuse the pun, I'd say that I was shocked.

I must have been four then. In another year or two I would say to my mother, "I don't want to pray that prayer," and she would say, "Well, pray your own words then, as long as you pray." And I would thank God that my sore had healed and that I didn't get hurt playing Tackle-ena in the backyard with my big brother's friends. In five years I would mock ditty prayers at the dinner table:

"Rub-a-dub-dub, thanks for the grub."

And would receive a proper scolding. In ten years I would take a principled stand against ditty prayers and begin to wonder how best to address God without the aid of rote memorization. What exactly was my heart? How could I speak from it? What did it have to say? What did God glimpse through my backtracks, my pauses, my changes of mind? What did he want me to pray? Was he listening? Did he answer? What was that echo? Was he there?

In twenty years, my wife would argue with her devout, simple mother: "No, Mother. The reason our daughter does not pray any bedtime prayers when she sleeps over is that we do not teach her those things. Why not? Because they don't mean anything, that's why. A parrot could pray them. No, it is not talking to God. It's playing a record. You made me pray those prayers when I was little and it turned me off to prayer. I was sixteen years old before I thought even once about what those words meant. We want our daughter to pray what she thinks and to think what she prays . . ."

And by now, I have banished "Now I Lay Me" so decisively from my life that I am amazed to find it so perfectly preserved, like a bug in amber, under a log in the back forty of my mind. What has it been doing there all this time? Have the words gone on praying without me?

Perhaps so. I recall a class I once took at a community art center. We were there to improve our imaginative intuition through visualization exercises. As we stretched out on our rugs, our teacher would turn out the lights and play cosmic-sounding electronic music. Then she would talk us slowly down into a light to moderately heavy trance and off on a mental journey among the ballets and forests and diamonds and snakes of our minds. I recall dimly only now that on the first night, as the lights went out and my head settled gingerly onto the rug, the words "Now I lay me down to sleep. I pray thee, Lord, my soul to keep . . ." spontaneously escaped from my mind like a long breath.

It seemed a reflex, a mistaken one, which I quickly corrected as I swung my mind around to the chore of utterly relaxing and letting visions flood my mind. But now I think with amusement about that reflex. Perhaps it was a real prayer, a spontaneous appeal from the heart for protection from a possible New Age swindle to which I was making myself vulnerable. Or was it no more than the salivation of Pavlov's dog?

Unlike my parents, who in their late sixties still kneel at their bedside in prayer before retiring, I do not kneel or utter formal prayers before bed. I speak formal prayers at other times. And yet every night when I rest my head upon my pillow, in some more or less obscure fashion I pray the Lord my soul to keep. This turning of the mind toward eternity and righteousness, the Creator and Redeemer of the world, the origin and destination of my soul, goes with

the shutting of my eyes. It is perhaps a reflex, but I never feel that
it is a mistake. In that moment I turn my back on the tyranny of
selfhood and the long fall into materialistic oblivion. In the dark,
behind my closed eyelids, I go to sleep prepared, expectant, facing
the sun.

Since I have stood so firmly against ditty prayers for so many years,
I am surprised at the traces of joy that accompany my recollection
of the words "Now I lay me down to sleep . . ." According to my joy,
there must have been more going on during those ancient recitals
than I have been willing to allow.

For many of my childhood years I had no understanding of the
words. I made some sounds in walking rhythm, which I've now
learned to call iambic tetrameter. The sounds felt good to make. *Keep*
sounded like *sleep,* and *take* sounded like *wake,* so it was easy to
remember all four lines (now I call them "rhyming couplets"). I
could do it!

Furthermore, my ditty prayer gave me a chance to spend some
moments with my mom or, some nights, my dad. I thought about the
little kids who didn't have moms or dads. I felt so lucky. Thank you
for moms and dads, God. Thank you for "quality time," for moments
of "bonding," for contexts for intimacy and processes of socialization.

Kneeling by my bed and talking to an invisible guy named "God"
seemed like the queerest thing in the world to do. I never would
have thought of doing it by myself. But Mom and Dad said it was
good to do. They trusted him. God must have been something like
Mom's mom or Dad's dad. And so I learned about hierarchical relationships, transcendence and mediation. I learned about generation-
al covenants from the inside.

Every night I had to pray that prayer. Once didn't take care of it
for good. And still, each time was plenty for that day. It was sort of
like the sun. The sunshine was plenty for each day, but the next day
we got some more. The sun was never through. It just went round
and round. So I learned that some things were good not because they
got better; they were good because they stayed the same. Rituals, I've

learned, are something like that: cyclic, redundant, dynamic, equilib-
rious. They counteract the slow erosions of time and become the loci
of enduring values.

Again, I think the first word I ever really thought about for long
was the word *die.* "If I should die before I wake"—the thought of
it! Shutting my eyes each night must be a huge risk. I was setting out
on a trip. I might not come back! If it weren't a real risk, Mom and
Dad probably wouldn't have made me pray about it. They were
scared I wouldn't come back, too, but they seemed to figure that
talking to this invisible guy "God" about it was the safe thing to do.
"If I should die before I wake, I pray thee, Lord, my soul to take."
If Mom and Dad and I could say that without throwing up from fear,
it must mean that dying wasn't the worst thing. Not having your soul
taken was. So I wanted to have my soul taken. Well, whatever happened, keeping or taking, God was the one doing it, so I figured I
was okay. I wondered whether God would take my soul even if I
forgot to pray the prayer. Did the prayer make him do it? Did you
have to ask first in order to get taken? Did anybody ever not want
their soul taken? And then did they not get taken? Anybody with half
an eye can see an incipient catechism here and possibly the seeds
of a systematic theology, both of which I am content never to have
written.

Only by the period between childhood and adolescence that ed-
ucators now sometimes refer to as "transescence," half a dozen years
after my first mumbling of those comforting words devoid of meaning, did I become self-conscious about the language of the prayer.
I realized one day in grammar class that the phrase "lay me down"
was obsolete and not concise. Today we would say "lie down," using
the intransitive verb "lie." Of course, that would blow the rhythm and
spoil the prayer's antique charm. Proof, I concluded, of the prayer's
irrelevance to modern lives.

One day I realized, too, that I had been saying "I pray *the* Lord . . ."
whereas the correct wording was "I pray *thee,* Lord." The prayer was
intended to be direct address to God, but not once in all my growing

years had I understood that. To whom then had my prayers been addressed? If not to God, then my self-proclaimed prayer was not actually a prayer. It was more like a report to my mother. The statement "I pray the Lord" had contradicted itself. Hence, it had been a lie. What had I done to my mind and my heart by kneeling every night to utter a lie? Did God consider my words a prayer anyway? What a muddle. And muddles were like puddles: best stepped over.

Still later, before I had heard of "speech act theory" and "elocutionary acts," I began to ask myself why any person in his or her right mind would allow an announcement of an action to constitute the action itself. Why say, "I pray"? Why not just pray: Lord, please keep my soul while I sleep. If a mosquito landed on my arm, would I say "Now I wave my hand to slap"? If I stood in front of a drinking fountain, would I say "Now I sway me down to slurp"? Surely not. I would slap and I would slurp—and I would pray. Real prayers, aimed at heaven, not public-service announcements.

By now, of course, I've learned that there is a way of saying the words "I pray" so that they mean "I beg" or "I beseech." Spoken with an honest intention, they not only mean *what* they say. They mean *as* they say. They mean *by the saying*. In this case, meaning isn't merely something the words have. It's something the speaker does. But I didn't know that when I was a caustic teenager, before my intelligence had begun to decline.

The point I missed was that the prayer had been a ceremony. It defined a time and a place. It gave me a structure. It set me in action. And once in a while, in that action, notwithstanding my hurry to scramble between the sheets, my intentions did in fact catch up with my speech and, fleetingly, I prayed, thoughts, words and actions all in tune.

Those fleeting moments, I believe, are some of the formative experiences of my life. And they are the real reason I am surprised by joy when the electrodes are charged and up from that three-pound pudding I call my brain floats the scene of a boy in his jammies singing the long-forgotten lyrics, "Now I lay me down to sleep . . ."

Should I teach my daughter rote prayers? This is the wrong time to ask. She's already a "transescent." But when she was seven, she returned from a sleepover at a friend's house. As I tucked her in bed that night, she looked up from her pillow and asked, "Do you want to hear my prayers?"

I thought.

"I'd be happy to hear you pray," I said, "and I'll pray with you. But what do you mean by 'your prayers'?" The poor kid had to have a semanticist for a father.

"Jill has a same prayer she says every night. And her mom listens to her."

"Well," I instructed, "I haven't taught you little prayers to say. I don't want you to get stuck in a rut. And I don't pray them, either. God knows what's in your heart. So why don't you just pray the words that come from there?"

I was magnificent, a champion of honesty and spontaneity. And she tried, like an angel, some words about her sores and her best friend and her Pound Puppy. Her prayer was beautiful and honest. But when I snapped off the light, I sensed from her breathing and her slow "Good night" that she was mildly disturbed. And so was I.

A little bit of joy had left her world.

# Don't Run in Church

O ne cast-iron syllable—"Boys!"—will stop a pack of running
boys in your average church narthex. Simple. No residue.
Same with flat commands like "Don't run," "Slow down" or
"Whoa there."

"Boys, boys" works smartly, too, though a kid worth his Reeboks
will catch the slightly imploring tone behind the commanding posture and will feel secretly empowered by it.

"Boys, boys, boys" will leave the little scalawags scoffing, "What's
*his* problem?" But they'll slow down, at least until they round a
corner. Not much mental, emotional, psychological, moral or spiritual residue there, either.

"Don't run in church" is a different matter. Thirty years after the
last time I was admonished with it, the phrase still rattles around in
my cranium. What did it tell me about running? What did it tell me
about church? What did it tell me about grown-ups? What did it tell
me about me? At the time, it told me nothing because I was not

reflective—Ronny and Greg were getting away! Nevertheless, *something* registered. Rather, I should say *some things* registered, because what stuck over the years, like mussels to a wharf, were the innumerable differences between people, their attitudes and their notions of church.

I can recall as many meanings of "Don't run in church" as there were people who said it. Listen to them all talking at once in the narthex of time:

Don't run in church. The floors are freshly buffed. You might slip and hurt your elbow, and I don't want that responsibility on my shoulders. There, you've been warned. You're on your own now. Don't come crying to me if you fall.

Don't run in church. I'm having a conversation here with Mrs. Melmac. Can't you see that I'm touching her elbow and we're trading proprieties?

Don't run in church. That's a rule. Rules are to be obeyed. If you run, you will break the rule. That would be wrong because it is wrong to break rules. If you stop running, you will be in compliance with the rule and will cease to be a consideration. That is what we want.

Don't run in church. This is God's house, and in it some magical things occur. If you fall while running, that will be God's way of punishing you. So don't run. I don't want to have to say "I told you so."

Don't run in church—at least, don't run where I can see you (wink, wink). I'm kind of a scamp myself, and I've hip-swiveled through many a lobby in my day. But I'm a grown-up now, and when you grow up you learn that lots of those obnoxious things grown-ups always said had a certain not completely unreasonable point behind them. I feel I should say "Don't run." But, golly, I wish I were your age.

Don't run in church. This is God's house, and we should respect it. The same would be true if you were at my house. Try to be polite to the host, because he has opened his home to us. Don't put your feet on the furniture, either. And get rid of that gum.

Don't run in church. Running is a release of energy, and energy is from the devil. Save it for Monday. On Sundays you should hold yourself thus, hands behind your back—shallow breathing—don't move your whole head, just your eyes.

Don't run in church. You have been told that before, and yet you run. Why? Willful disobedience, that's what it is. Willful disobedience welling up out of your proud, your black little heart. One more display of evil mockery like that and I shall be forced to pinch your neck, just as I pinched the neck of that Wallace boy who wasted all the towels in the men's room. Nobody officially appointed me to be your policeman, but this is my little contribution.

Don't run in church. God is a very temperamental sort of guy. When you run, you create sound waves—vibrations, really. God is sort of like a delicate bird. Too many vibrations and you might rattle him right off his perch. See, he's really hoping to get all the praise he can out of these people, and if you run, you see, you may wreck the whole thing for him. He won't have a good Sunday. And then we'll have a whole week before we get to boost him up again. Who knows what may happen to God during that time?

Don't run in church. The floors are freshly buffed. You might slip and crack your elbow. You know, I value your health as much as I value my own and would feel your pain as if it were mine. Restrain your beautiful urge to run as I restrain mine so that we both may remain happy, strong and full of praise to God, who would probably also want to run in church if he were here in his sneakers.

# God's Temples

F ranklin?

*Uh-oh. When he calls me "Franklin" he usually wants to talk about report cards, or religion, or some bodily function.*

Mind if I come into your room? How about if you put down that joystick for a minute so you and I can have a little talk?

*I think best in digital mode. TZIW TZIW tinka tinka TZIW TZIW SPBLAW blblbl*

Franklin, just shut off the Nintendo so we don't have to talk above the racket. Your mother offered to join us, but I said, "I think Frankie and I need have a little man-to-man for once . . .

*I knew it. Bodily functions.*

He's getting to be—". . . I mean, you're getting to be a man, you know.

*Yeah, right. Remember that next time I ask to stay out late.*

I mean, have you noticed what I'm saying? Have you noticed anything

. . . *different* about yourself lately?

*Does he mean, like, how I study the underwear ads? Like how my armpits reek? Like how I practice making out with my pillow at night? No, I haven't noticed anything.*

I'm talking about . . . I'm talking about your body. That, and your voice, which may start breaking soon, and your emotions,

*Like, boredom?*

and your hair,

*Something wrong with my ponytail?*

you know, your hair, if you get my drift.

*Oh, that hair. Gee, get a life, Dad. I'm on the case. I've been watching. So far no action. Hm, I wonder if something's, like, seriously wrong.*

Won't be long and you'll be shaving. All that kind of stuff. Maybe you'd rather not talk about it.

*Not with you.*

I understand that. When I was a boy, I didn't much want to talk about it, either. I thought I was probably the only one in the world who was having, you know, those new kinds of thoughts.

*Yeah, like about Ferraris and Michael Jordan?*

And my dad—sheesh, my dad. I swore I'd never be like him. He was a farmer and so scared to talk to anyone about all the really important facts of, you know, life and stuff.

*Good, Dad. Fortunately, you don't have a problem with talking.*

He had me out by the hogpen watching the shoats—they're about like you, you know, young—and one would stand there with his front hooves up on another's back, the way pigs sometimes do—I suppose you can about picture that.

*Like the quarterback when we play football. Oh yeah, I can picture that. I can about hear it, too. And smell it. Great picture, Dad. That's exactly how I want it to be when I get married.*

Farm boys see the earthy side of procreation all the time.

*Procreation? Is that like recreation?*

But the pigs weren't actually, you know, doing anything . . . abnormal.

*Oh no. Course not.*

Just practicing.

*Right. Just practicing. So it's okay if I practice?*

I hope my frankness isn't upsetting you . . .

*Oh yeah, right, Dad. I'm going to be upset about some pigs. And every time I see a pair of flies doing it I'm gonna start trembling and ask to leave the room. I'll have to have counseling every time I watch reruns of "Three's Company."*

Anyway, he'd say, my dad would say, "Get a good eyeful of that now, son. You ain't no different. You can learn a lot about life down on the farm. Right there's where it all starts."

*About that time, I'd be thinking about frying up some bacon.*

What I'm trying to say, kiddo, and maybe I'm not coming up with exactly the right words, but what I'm trying to say is that your body, you know, legs, arms,

*Yeah, yeah, I know the one*

everything, if you know what I mean, it's like a *temple*.

*Whoa! Whoa! Whoa! Where does this "temple" stuff come in?*

And, and . . . I don't mean just *your* body, either. I'm talking about a girl's body, too. Everybody's changing real fast about now . . . I suppose maybe you've caught on to some of that.

*Well, yeah. Me and the guys call it the T-Shirt Patrol. We've got every girl sized. I suppose those are steeples we're looking at. I'm sorry. I'm not getting into this "temple" thing.*

But that's a, you know, a whole nother subject. Your mom would probably have some words on that. It's a temple of the Holy Spirit, is what I'm trying to say.

*Oh, man, that cleared things up.*

When my parents gave me a book about the facts of life, it was called *God's Temples.*

*Spare me that one, along with the instruction book on how to crank your Model T.*

I didn't make the connection at first.

*Well, hey! Maybe your body doesn't feel much like stones and stained glass, either.*

But the Bible says your body is not your own. It belongs to God, who bought it at a price.

*If I want a sex manual, I don't think I'll be picking up the Bible.*

So you should honor God with your body. Something like that. Get it?

*Yeah, like I'm getting a headache.*

Well, I mean, take your mom and me.

*Please!*

Well, actually, there's a lot of stuff there I wouldn't want to get into, not at your age, anyway—well, not *ever,* really. It's completely our business, and we'll protect that in the sanctity of our matrimonial, uh, um, oh, what's the word?

*Muddle?*

Anyway, I just have to ask you to respect that. Don't get me wrong. I can't expect you to be completely without curiosity, you know. That's one of those things. Just so you don't start going around peeking through keyholes or making stethoscopes out of Dixie cups and holding 'em up to the wall or anything.

*I should tell him. I stopped doing that years ago. It was too boring. All I heard were arguments about money. I've been thinking about some electronic hookups I saw in a magazine. Figure maybe I haven't been staying up late enough for the real action. I could use a small receiver dish. Run a line to a recorder in my bedroom. I could get a good night's sleep and check the tapes in the morning. Who knows? If I get some good action, I could rig up a video camcorder. Little fiber optic lens sewed into the drapes? Totally invisible. I could have a gang here for a sleepover, and we could watch reruns out in our tent. Awesome. I could tell him we were watching Benji.*

I admit, I did that when I was your age, or maybe a little older. I did some pretty crazy stuff. But there you go. That was the old man's fault. He never told me anything. And that's why I'm having this little heart-to-heart with you now. You understand? Well, anyway, take your mom and me.

*I don't need to. I'm stuck with these wasteoids.*

I'm going to be completely frank with you. Not to upset you or anything but because I think a dad owes it to his son to pass on the important things he knows.

*If he wanted to pass on something really important, he could start with an allowance.*

Your mother and I, I mean, we, that is to say, you . . . may have thought that you just . . . happened.

*Yeah, I used to think that—when I was in first grade! What does this guy take me for? I probably know more dirty words than he does. I know all about women. Give me five minutes and I could be looking at a magazine that would show me the whole works. He'd never find out. And we had a class on safe sex at school. I know how AIDS is transmitted. He probably doesn't. I read in the encyclopedia all about PMS and mammary glands and ejaculation. I know that choking the chicken doesn't make you blind. My friend Gerald told me all about that. So I'm supposed to think babies just happen? I'm sure!*

Do you see what I'm driving at?

*A brick wall?*

That you just . . . happened. Well, that's not quite the case. No, no. Not at all. You don't just "happen." Do you understand me, Frankie? Look at me.

*I can't. Okay, I'll try. No, I can't. I'll lose it.*

This is crucial: you don't just *happen.* No, no. There's *quite* a bit more to it than that. You'd be surprised. In fact, maybe you're already starting to catch a little bit of this. I'm not sure what you're hearing on the street—all those kids with their dirty jokes—don't listen to that garbage, boy. You're gonna learn the wrong words for everything, and still not know what it takes to make a baby.

*Okay. I'll play along. What he doesn't know won't hurt him.*

It takes at least two. *Exactly* two, I mean. That's how we're made. But that's the point I've been coming around to. God made us beautiful.

Don't ever, ever feel that you have to be ashamed of the way you feel,
> *Who said I did? I feel like a stud.*

or the way you're made, or if you feel something funny going on, you know, when some girl your age winks at you in class, and she's got that wide-eyed innocent look, and she's gorgeous?
> *Oh, please.*

And she's wearing these pink slouch socks, brand new,
> *Oh, please!*

and you think she looks so great? you know? And she's chewing on the end of her pencil?
> *Dad, Dad. You're outta touch. We don't even use pencils. We're at the computers.*

And she's twirling her hair? Don't worry, those feelings are coming. And wham! You're gonna be hit so hard.
> *Whoopee.*

The point being, your body is a *temple.*
> *I suppose now he's gonna start talking about steeples.*

You gotta grasp that concept. And don't let go. It'll take you through all the problems.
> *How did this doofus ever have me?*

In fact, I'm going to tell you something about your mother and me. Something I never told you before and something I'm sure you never saw. It's probably about the most secret thing I could tell you, but I don't mind. This is our time, right Big Guy?
> *Oh, no, I think I'm going to hurl.*

And it's not easy, I know, but we're learning some really important stuff here. Well, before we, that is, your mother and I, turn in for the night,
> *I don't want to hear this!*

it doesn't matter what we're planning on, maybe nothing at all, most times,
> *Don't go into it.*

but we both get down on our knees and pray.
> *Huh?*

Bet you didn't know that. Do those two things seem strange together?

*What? Praying and then going at it in bed? I'd say so.*

Huh? Does that seem strange? Do you know what I'm saying? I suppose they do because that's not the way you see it in the movies. But that's the point I'm getting at. You get it? Both of us are temples, and when we get in under the sheets, we're still temples.

*I don't really want to see this.*

In each other's arms. Yep. Temples of the Holy Spirit. Temples in the sight of the Lord. Maybe it's hard to picture that.

*I'm given up trying. This is making me mad. I haven't even had sex yet and I'm already losing my appetite for it.*

I was talking to the preacher about this and he told me something I never knew. He said the New Testament word for temple really means "tabernacle." And you know what a tabernacle was? It was a tent. The ancient Israelites had their temple in a tent.

*So I suppose we're going to move all the Israelites under the sheets with us now?*

And they moved it from place to place with them wherever they went. See that? Your body is like a tent. It's a temporary dwelling, as long as you're on earth.

*That's mildly interesting.*

But inside the tent was a place they called the Holy of Holies. That was a place behind a veil where God would dwell. See that? That's what I mean, your body is a temple. It's like a tabernacle. Inside, there's room for the Holy Spirit. That's why I wouldn't want you to abuse your body in any way. Because when you treat yourself carelessly, you do the same thing to the Holy Spirit.

*That's the one decent thing he's said so far.*

That's what I've been getting at. That's where babies come from. The Holy of Holies. Yep. The Holy of Holies. Maybe I'm not saying it right. Oh well. Maybe you get what I'm saying.

*I think I'm losing it. What Holy of Holies are we talking about?*

Hey, Chum.

*I can't decide which is worse: "Chum" or "Big Guy." I think it's "Big*

*Guy." Yeah. Definitely, it's "Big Guy." I hate this part where the dad's all mooshy because he's dropped his pants for the world to see. Gerald said his dad was the same way when he gave the big sex talk. He kept calling Gerald "Son" until Gerald said, "What,* Father?"

I can't believe how much ground we've covered in a few short minutes. I feel great about this. I wish my dad had done the same for me. Always talk it over. That's what I recommend.

*Yeah, Dad. Gee. I'm all talked out.*

You're not saying much. Franklin. You got any questions? No? Well, I just want you to know that if you ever have any questions, you can always come to me.

"Yeah, Dad. I got a question. You want to play a game of Nintendo? I'll waste ya."

# God Sees You

Y ou know how the thing you should have said always comes to mind *afterwards?* Well, only now does it occur to me what I might have said more than thirty years ago when one of those finger-wagging adults tried to keep me from mischief with the warning "Remember, God sees you."

I can see it now. At those words, I would have looked up from my cowlick in the long grass behind the garage, rolling the cigarette butt between thumb and fingers until fresh tobacco squirted out the end, then clearing and spitting to dissociate myself from the sin of smoking it. The half-body peering at me from around the corner would not need to know that I had picked up the cigarette at the tennis court, half-smoked and romantically—stirringly!—imprinted with lipstick.

"With all due respect to you and to God," I would have said, "what are you saying? Hardly anyone who believes in an omniscient Creator would disagree with your statement *qua* theological proposition. In fact, because the predicate is already implied in the very definition of the word *God,* your statement should be ruled a tautology. Shall I presume, then, that you are not concerned with the propositional truth of the statement but rather with the act you perform in uttering it, namely the act of admonishing or adjuring? That is all very well, and you may rest assured that as your obedient child I submit to your admonitions, ordinarily. Nevertheless, in the terms of your statement I detect a certain equivocation on the word *sees* which prevents me from acting immediately in accordance with your wishes. Don't we habitually assume an analogy between God's parentage of the human race and humans' parentage of their offspring? As you stand there with arms akimbo, under the hornet-sheltering eaves, having approached surreptitiously, it is difficult for me not to suppose that you draw a parallel between God's manner of seeing and your own. Perhaps, then, you intended to say, 'God *spies* you.' But spying, it seems to me, is a most ungodlike thing to do. A spy is an intelligence-gathering agent in the service of a superior. What further intelligence could God need, and who is his superior? But perhaps when you said 'God sees you' you had in mind something more like the Orwellian nightmare of Big Brother. An all-powerful inquisitor and judge with an eye poking into every public and private place. A totalitarian whom history will devour unless he devours it first. I think too highly of you to believe that you would fall prey to such a cynical and paranoid fancy, although at times a child like me has to wonder. I'll be honest. When I hear 'God sees you,' I interpret that as 'God *notices* you.' And, I'll be honest some more: being noticed doesn't sound all bad, not when my parents are busy all day toting briefcases and pushing carpet sweepers and ignoring my Friday Folder. I don't mean to criticize you, but I can salvage some comfort from the words 'God sees you,' even if comfort was not exactly what you had intended to convey. Moreover, if I take seriously what you've taught me about God since I was small enough to ride horsey on your ankle, I have to conclude that God sees more than just my youthful indiscretions like this one here behind the garage. He sees my coming and my going, my night sweats and my daydreams, my acts of mercy and my tears when abused. He strengthens my bones and softens my glance, feels my wants and knows my needs. He reads words in books through my eyes and speaks their message to my heart. And when I light up a discarded, half-smoked cigarette behind the garage, he sees—and *knows*—my fascination with the head of flame on the stolen match, my boyish yearning for the woman whose lips embraced this charcoal filter, my impatience to be big, my satisfaction with the bitingly dark aroma of tobacco. He sees all my wants as symptoms of my blind reception of the power with which he draws me to himself.

"So you see, there's tonal ambiguity in your statement that God sees me. Consequently, I'm not sure I know exactly how to respond . . ."

I could go on with what I *should* have said. But as I was saying, we always think up the best comebacks when it's too late. Oh well, maybe it's just as well I couldn't have come up with the perfect words when I was eight. They would have landed me a seat in the corner, for sure.

# If Jesus Would Return Right Now

A nn Landers, at least in one of the apocryphal stories that surround her, is well known for advising people always to wear clean underpants. Imagine wearing some sagging, spotty, shot-up pair and then, nightmare of nightmares, being badly mangled in a car crash. The medics might have to cut off your pants to save your life, and there, in front of all those onlookers, your dirty secret would be exposed. THEN HOW WOULD YOU FEEL?

Pretty ashamed, I guess. I suppose that would pretty much rule out running for high office.

The religious equivalent of this folk wisdom is the rhetorical question "What if Jesus would return right now?" The question implicitly refers to Christ's Second Coming, the cosmological and moral equivalent of a head-on collision, vividly described by Jesus in Matthew 24 as a time of wars and false prophets, famines and earthquakes, a time dreadful for women with child and nursing mothers. The searchlight of eternity would freeze you in its glare, that's what. As the kids in my neighborhood today might say, "You're toast."

There are pockets of, let's just call it, "neighborly concern" in the American countryside where you might still find this question trumpeted on billboards, wrenching the consciences—if not the steering wheels—of passing motorists. The chief use of the question, however, has been for the moral correction of children, especially for the purpose of scaring them away from worldly amusements. "What if Jesus would return while you were at a dirty movie?" the parents of my generation liked to ask. Their parents would have said "at a movie," period. What if he should return while you were making out, or playing cards, or dancing, or burning June bugs with your magnifying glass? Had we as a generation had the presence of mind, we would have retorted: What if he returns while you're committing adultery?

These were parents who also told their children that Jesus knew their every weakness, that every deed was recorded in the Book of Life, that God was watching over them every moment of every day. The kids could be sure that if they were found sinning, it would come as no surprise to God. Is it any wonder that they kept going to movies anyway, albeit with a few wary glances toward the exits, should Jesus' peeping head be silhouetted there?

Those kids didn't know any theology, but they were experts in theological inconsistency. Though the Protestant kids hadn't the words for it, they knew that their kind didn't accept that Catholic stuff about being safely in a state of grace at the moment of death—the kind of superstition that prevented Hamlet from stabbing his stepfather, Claudius, as the villain knelt in prayer. Therefore, being "caught in sin" would not be the mortal error their theologically opportunistic parents were making it out to be. In fact, if they were listening with even one ear cocked during Sunday school, they were probably catching wind of the notion that their "best works were as filthy rags." That "in Adam's Fall, we sinned all." That we humans, to the last unit, are "totally depraved" and that "all have sinned and fall short of the glory of God." At the time, they may not have believed all those

incriminations of the human heart, but they were smart enough to
see that, theologically speaking, it trumped the hand their parents
were playing: "If Jesus would return right now." So they went with
the winning hand and took in a movie.

I'm not defending those kids in the theaters, the ones "playing
doctor," the ones shooting craps, the ones watching "Soul Train," the
ones with dirty underwear—or even the ones with clean underwear
sitting up straight in Sunday school. We—I'll include myself—could
be naughty. Tricky. Sleazy. Dirty. Two-faced. Mean. Insincere. All the
worst things that can be said of children. And we could be charming,
sweet, well-scrubbed, obedient, cheerful—thin slices of heaven.

But we, in our worldly youth, so busy underestimating both the
threat and the promise of Jesus' return, were not as utterly wrong as
our pious parents made us out to be. However, I have no word for
the smidgen of virtue we possessed. So I'll invent one:

Imbelief.

*Imbelief* means not-belief. It is not to be confused with *unbelief*.
Remember, for a moment, the words of the father who brought his
son to Jesus to be healed of an evil spirit. Jesus told him that "everything is possible for him who believes." "I do believe," said the
father; "help me overcome my unbelief" (Mk 9:23-24). Unbelief is
failure to believe in a manifest truth; in its absolute form, it is resolute
failure to believe in a saving truth. And from the point of view of a
believer, it's a great vice.

Imbelief, on the other hand, is refusal to take refuge in a falsehood
or half-truth. Whereas unbelief in a truth is a vice, imbelief in a
falsehood is a virtue, though not nearly so great a virtue as belief in
a truth. Sometimes, in fact, I would argue, imbelief may be the only
soil in which belief can flower.

I don't know what's become of all the kids who heard the tinny
tune of their parents' otherworldly pietism and weren't led that way.
I congratulate them on their imbelief, if such it was. Some of them
may be sitting in front of their TV sets right now, scratching their
necks. Some may be living lives of crime, just as their parents feared,

only worse. Some may have translated their vices into professions and so made their parents and communities proud. I can't account for the holiness of their "underwear" today. But I hope—and here I reveal the Reformed coloration of my thinking—I hope some of those kids have grown beyond imbelief, grown up, let's just say, to make the movies, not only to watch them. To make movies dedicated to the glory, not of a God who goes "BOO!" in crowded theaters, but of one who put the first people in a garden and expected them to cultivate.

# Everybody Just Pray to Yourselves

*T*hat Norman Rockwell family with heads bowed serenely in the booth by the wall was mine. I was the one with my thumb in my eye, making like I had an itch as I put in my moment of silence. While the mom and dad took painfully long with their "thine is the kingdoms and the powers," I was the one looking around discreetly, rearranging my silverware.

Now, my childhood was free of major embarrassments. I had two parents—the two you saw with me in the restaurant—who loved each other and let it show. No alcoholics or crooks among the relations, no madness, just ministers, farmers, housewives, successful businessmen. I spent seventeen years in the same two-story stucco house by a college. Never ran into trouble with the law. Played football, baseball, tennis, basketball, in season. Built ice rinks in the backyard, miniature golf courses in the garden. Played "Five Dollars" in the street with my brothers and the neighborhood dirtballs. Raked elm leaves, burned them at the curb and rode bikes through the curtains of smoke. Lots of bruises, a few proud sprains, no bad breaks.

But somewhere in that childhood idyll I contracted shame. It might have been right there in that restaurant where you saw me. Maybe you thought we came there often; I thought the same about you. But our six-member family hardly ever went to a sit-down place. The time you saw me might have been my first. Our usual, if we had one, was to hunker in a two-door Ford at a place called Robby's where we nibbled at hamburgers flat as potholders, 19 cents apiece, sucked on strawberry shakes till the paper straws collapsed, and fought over who spilled ketchup on the transmission hump. That was our element then. Dabbing at salt with licked fingers, elbows in each other's ears, passing paper napkins, begging unsuccessfully for seconds.

None of that was allowed at the restaurant table. We had to leave our dirty knees and cloud fantasies outside. Instead, our private family selves peered through the window. We saw how people looked sitting in a restaurant; thought how we might look sitting that way; made new selves of what we saw; stepped into those selves; and walked in through the door. From then until we walked back past the cash register, we little brothers and one sister studied at the school of etiquette. We fought only with our ankles. We ordered within our father's means. We made high-pitched exclamations over standard cheesecake. And when we walked out that restaurant door, our private family selves, we found, had grown impatient and padded off. They would greet us at home as we pulled into the driveway, tails wagging.

Was our secret imposture not shame enough?

No. You saw me in the clutch of even deeper shame. After the waitress left with our orders, we spent the next interval swiping at smudges, doodling on place mats and looking around. When the plates arrived, pools of turkey gravy steaming, unexpected servings of carrot cubes and peas prompting us to ask, "Mom, do we have to eat those?" as we argued *sotto voce* over whose roll was whose, many heads, including yours, turned to look.

Had we been at home, my father would have said, "Fold your
hands. Close your eyes. Let's pray." In a sonorous voice reserved for
praying and defining words, he would have enumerated the world's
ills and the stages of God's redemptive plan, borrowing both structure and phraseology from the Heidelberg Catechism, would have
risen on oratorical wings toward a quotation of lines from a favorite
hymn and ended with a family health survey, as our gravy congealed
and our peas puckered. There in the restaurant, however, as we
prepared to saw our turkey slabs, he laid down his implements,
glanced around and said to us, gently, as if making an allowance, and
regretfully, as if he blamed himself for squandering the dead-air time
when the waitress had been off in the kitchen: "Everybody just pray
to yourselves."

That's when you saw me. I was praying, for real, asking for forgiveness of my many sins and giving thanks for the food so graciously
set before me—working up my feelings to the melody of borrowed
phrases. But at the same time, feigning eye fatigue and reluctant to
bow, I was enmeshed in confused self-awareness. As at home, Dad
gave and withheld privileges. As at home, it was good and right to
be Christian and necessary to do the thing of praying before meals,
even if eyes were staring. In true evangelical fashion, it was taking
a stand. Making a testimony. And yet, in praying "to ourselves," we
weren't exactly trying to look Christian. We were allowing ourselves
to be seen trying not to look *too* Christian. In deference to the air
of the marketplace, we were trying not to be obnoxious.

I didn't like your curious glance and didn't want to pray aloud in
front of you. Yet when Dad granted us the reprieve, I felt strange
uneasiness within my relief. My maternal grandfather was a minister,
and a bold one. He would have prayed aloud, stirringly, in his pulpit
voice, so that the whole restaurant would have heard and been
moved, and I would have been embarrassed half to death, but within
my embarrassment I would have been thrilled by the half-crazy display. Though I complied with my father, I wasn't with him either in
the desire to pray or in the desire to draw a cone of silence around

us. Both my impiety and my piety were tuned to my grandfather's recklessness. He embarrassed me, and that impressed me.

Quite a number of years went by before I could see the added irony in the phrase "Everybody just pray to yourselves." Taken literally it meant, "Don't pray to God. You can't get there from here. Just pray to your selves." How appropriate that meaning seemed for a faintly craven family in a restaurant, praying out of the corner of its eyes. My wife tells me, too, that years ago, if her mother and father had argued before dinner, they would pull up their chairs, faces bitter and flushed, still dutiful toward their Lord but in the dirt with one another, and her mother would mutter—you guessed it: "Everybody can just pray to yourself."

What's to be learned? Maybe this, that guilty prayers, like cold-air balloons, don't rise.

# Say Grace

*T*here is a dog in me that whines and leaps at my feeding dish. I say this with no disrespect for dogs. A dog, by nature, is a yearning machine. When its master walks in at feeding time, its nose and ears, every muscle, every hair and every claw can read the signs: morning sunshine, birds, footsteps, kitchen cupboard, whistle, "Here boy," can opener, yeah, yeah . . . snap, kill, gorge! And as the body takes in circumstantial signs, the *eye* fixes desperately and without mercy on the prize: beef chunks in gravy! When a dog falls to without so much as a murmured please or thanks, he does a perfectly doggy thing.

I have that same dog in me, impatient to devour. I'm not ashamed of it. It marks me as the creature that I am. But what I do at meals no dog would ever do. I whisper "Down, boy" to my hunger; then I pray. Over corn chips and carrot sticks in a lunchroom. Around the Thanksgiving spread with all the relatives. Furtively in a restaurant. Stop, I say. I will conduct a short ceremony now. For reasons that I feel, this ceremony at this moment is more important to me than chowing down.

What's going on here?

Some anthropologists trace the ritual pause for prayer far back in history to a time before we learned to cultivate crops. Eons before pasteurization or refrigeration, when we were still nomads and hunters and scavengers, we had little control over the quality of foods we ate. The next odd mushroom, berry or shred of blue meat could strike us dead. Under those circumstances, we were wise to call for a god's help before risking a meal. Why not? A moment of beseeching in bug-eyed terror was a small premium to pay for term life insurance. When at last we became agrarian and our larders began to overflow, premeal oblations could become prayers of thanksgiving.

Today, in a hundred variations, we still fold our paws. We call our ritual "saying grace." No dog has ever done it. But let this be said as well: no dog would ever continue to perform an action with such confusion of purpose as most of us have when we say grace.

Our purposes range from sacred to profane. Some people, with true piety, acknowledge that they have not personally raised the steak or grown the beans or known the gobleted water in its secret places in the earth. Feeling thankful, unworthy and supernaturally sustained, they pause to acknowledge that which lies beyond themselves and to adore the author of all good things. Others, by training, simply feel guilty unless they have uttered a ritual prayer full of time-tested oral formulas: "bless this food unto our bodies . . . accept our thanks for this, thy bounty . . . blessings of which we are unworthy . . . missionaries on the foreign fields, blah blah." Others have a prayer-shaped gap in their consciences and fill it with brief words of homage to bounty, clutter, social contact and the power of animal appetite; they toss out their hands and exclaim, "Well, everybody, *enjoy!*" or "Let's eat!"

We're confused. We don't know what we're doing. We "say grace," but we don't know whom we're talking to, what we're saying or why. So we take it every way we can. Need evidence? Watch the guy who beams and says "Let's eat!" After the word "eat," his hands clap together like Albrecht Dürer's classic etching *Praying Hands*—check your knickknack shelf, you may have a bronze knockoff of it there. But then, watch, watch closely as his hands rub together ever so slightly, like fingers itching for the spoils. Thank you, O God; dive in, everybody. Prayer and predation. Grace and grab. In a mixed-up world, we'll take both.

And see that guy in the restaurant? When the food is set before him, watch how the sudden need to smooth a wrinkle in the napkin on his lap gives him a pretext for bowing his head. When he raises his head, not to be thought bowing, notice how the urge to itch his left eyelid gives him an excuse to keep his eyes closed as he continues saying grace. And before the last obligatory phrases are said and the eyes have lazed open upon the Amen, watch his body sway and his hands begin to nudge the silverware. He looks like someone who doesn't want to be observed praying but who can't resist doing it, like someone who sneaks through a pants pocket to scratch his groin.

Isn't he nonchalant? Isn't he tricky? Isn't he pathetic? You'd have to be a spy to catch him in the act. But I know his ways because I am describing myself in restaurants, in some of the weakest moments of my life. And I suspect I'm not alone.

The emptiness of our habits has not been lost on Hollywood. In two hit movies over Christmas 1991, saying grace became a joke. In *My Girl* Jamie Lee Curtis kicks off a meal with the bright-eyed cheer: "Rub-a-dub-dub, thanks for the grub. Yea, God!" In the Stephen Spielberg blockbuster *Hook*, Peter Pan (Robin Williams) sits down to a feast with the "lost boys" in Neverland and says to them, "Why don't we say grace?" All the boys turn to him and shout, "Grace!"

The amazing thing is not the temerity of such gags but rather the timidity. They are not the least bit original. They are simply meant to evoke universal recognition.

The phrase "say grace" has not always invited derision. The earliest English mention of saying grace before meals appears in a Middle English tract (c. A.D. 1225) called the *Ancren Riwle,* which gives advice to three young women about to become religious recluses. In 1526 William Tyndale used the phrase "sayd grace" in his translation of Matthew 26:30, a passage referring to Christ's singing psalms or hymns with his disciples following the Last Supper. Until then, to "say grace" meant to worship sincerely at a meal. In our times, however, the phrase has come to no good.

The difference between saying grace and genuine praying before a meal struck me most memorably at a recent summer institute for teachers. On our final day, we were gathered around tables for a catered luncheon. Since we were meeting under the auspices of a public university, there was no place among us for avowed religion. Moreover, in terms of religious persuasion we were a real bridge mix. Our leader and several of the teachers were Jewish. One elementary teacher (from Bolivia) practiced Native American religions. A sweet, soulful-eyed mystic who named herself "Buffalo Lady" spoke of a past life munching Big Blue Stem on the Great Plains, her spirituality a blend of New Age and Old West. A beautiful, Boston-bred sixties-style gypsy read us an autobiographical story about the Cucumber Man from Jupiter and a panel of miniature Indian wise men who played tricks on her mind. One woman said she was in the process of becoming a Christian but hadn't committed herself yet. Another, known for her radiant smile, said she was "born in the pew" in an Assemblies of God church. Another had been born in the pew but now, chain-smoking and black-leather-clad, was trying to chop all that out of her life with an ax. I'm sure there were some Episcopalians and Catholics in the group, but they didn't much talk about it.

To my surprise, the leader began the luncheon by saying, "Why don't we say some kind of grace? Here, let's hold hands." We lifted and clasped warm hands. We had spent five intense but fun weeks together, and now many amperes of mutual affection flowed through that live human wire over the ohms of our embarrassment. We listened with open eyes to words that were some kind of prayer addressed to our better human nature. Something on this order: "We have much to be thankful for after five weeks together, for all the friendships we've formed and the discoveries we've made. Let's be glad for each other, and this day, and the delicious food we're about to eat." There were murmured Amens all around the room as we let down our wire and fell to with forks and knives.

To those of a secular mind, saying any kind of grace may have seemed embarrassingly anachronistic. To those with religious rearing, I dare say, it seemed a fudge. Nevertheless, everyone appeared to appreciate the moment as a grace in the broadest sense of the word, that is, as a civilized refinement in our behavior and as a sharing of mutual blessings. Whatever our feelings, we kept them all inside.

I was thankful that day for both the form and the sentiment. We made the dog wait. And we honored each other. But it seems to me that saying grace ought to be more than that if it is to be anything more than a joke or a civil parody of religion. We need not simply leash our appetites. Instead, we ought to do a perfectly *godly* thing— read the Master's walk, hunger for eternity as a dog for its bowl, and chow down.

# Bless You

*I* cadt talk for log because by dose is bessed up. But sidce I'b od the verge of sdeezig adyway, this is probably as good a tibe as ady to wodder aloud: why do people always say "bless you" after sobebody has sdeezed? Baybe whed I'b through with by expladatiods, this torbedtig thig will fidally get here, add I'll sdeeze, add thed you cad bless be with full dowledge of what you're doig.

Ibagide you're a cavebad or a prehistorical agrariad type. You've dever heard of gerbs. Id fact, you've dever eved thought about the idside of your body. Your edebies are out there: hailstodes, wolves, lightdig, other cavebed. You cad see theb with your eyes, sbell theb with your dose—udless your cold is as bad as bide—hear theb with your ears add so od. Daturally, you'd thidk that the essedce of your life, your ibbortal soul, hug aroudd id your head, where all the sedsatiods were.

Ibagide, thed, that you suddedly had to sdeeze. Wouldd't you fear that everythig you stood for, all your bebories, all your dreabs, all your bystical ebpathy with the udiverse of datural thigs would go sprayig out the holes id the cedter of your face if you failed to cover your dose add bouth? I cad well ibagide that if you had a god dabed Bud-Y-Zur or sobethig awesobe-souddig like that, add if you had forgetted to cover up your last sdeeze, you would probably call out id fear: "Save be, Bud-Y-Zur! Let dot by braids be thus spewed id a bassive, udforeseed hachoo!"

Dow let's hop forward about ted thousad years to the fourth cedtury B.C. Here we would see Aristotle add Hippocrates fidally gettig the right idea. "A sdeeze," Hippocrates would say id a lecture to the world's first class of bedical studedts, "is the body's way of shoutig 'I badish thee!' to idvisible barbariads who have idvaded the dose.

"Thus," he would codtidue, wavig his chalk chuck, "our adcestors, who lived id igdoradce, had it just backwards. Sdeezig is dot bad but good. Id fact, it is essedtial to the health of the body. Let us all, thed, sdeeze as buch as we cad. Add whed a fellow citized has edjoyed a particularly fide sdeeze, let us sedd od high our praise to Zeus, sayig, 'Praises be for this bost excellent catharsis frob thy divide hadd, our Father and bost bagdificedt Sod of Tibe.' "

Dow jupp forward adother thousad years to the sixth cedtury A.D., durig the reigd of Pope Gregory the Great. All through Italy people are dyig of a biserable plague. Ode of the bady sybtobs of odcobing disease is violedt sdeezig. This is do ordidary flu bug goig aroud, what sobe people bight call the "crud." This is serious edough to call for divide idtervedtion. So by papal decree, those who forberly would have said "Edjoy good health" dow had to say "God bless you" to a sdeezer. Christiad sedtibent thus took od the force of a papal decree. Ibagide your life haggig so buch id the baladce that a sdeeze could upset it add a sibple bedidictiod could save it. Scary stuff, plagues.

That's how it's beed ever sidce. Dow, every tibe we sdeeze id public we recapitulate the whole history of sdeezig. You bay be od a bus whed a tidy wild hair starts twiddlig id your siduses sobewhere.

Your dose curls up like a Doberbad pidscher's add you bake little huckig soudds. Thed the guy id frodt of you will yell, "Dod't do it!" add bake like he's divig id a foxhole.

That's the cavebad era.

Thed the dice lady beside you will say, "Oh, go ahead, dear. It's neber good to hold theb back."

That's Aristotle add Hippocrates.

Add fidally, you'll let fly. It could be a dapalb bobb type of sdeeze or it could be just a little steab whistle. Do batter. Whed it's over, every head od the bus will swig aroudd your way add say id chorus: "God bless you . . . Bless you . . . Bless you."

That's Pope Gregory. Oh by . . . by dose.

As I was sayig, we go od blessig each other, day by day, without the slightest dotion of why we do it. But we wouldd't feel right dot doig it. We'd feel vulderable or hexed. That's the way superstitiods work—oh doh. Pardod be. I thidk I'b goig to—just a secod—here it cobes—just a secod—oh doh—oh doh—

# Happy Easter

B ecause it celebrates the cracking of the egg of cosmic gloom—the first and only self-willed resurrection from the dead!—Easter ought to be the very most exuberant of days. And as celebrated by Christians everywhere, it is a joyful time. Worshipers greet the dawn from riverbanks and hills. Big churches flash their brass ensembles, and the Orthodox, in ritualistic dialogue, exclaim: "Christ is risen!" "He is risen indeed!" Alleluias top off narratives of an empty tomb, and silky descants popple through the skies. Easter is a time of ecumenical expansiveness, too, as many Christians feast on paschal lamb and simulate Passover rituals for the instruction of their children. And as if the religious celebrations weren't enough, there are those marshmallow bunnies, those dyed eggs, those hunts, those bonnets and all that chocolate.

Has it struck you, then, that many Christians seem to have no popular salutation equal to the day? Imagine you are Peter or John, hotfooting it to the empty tomb. Or imagine that a glowing man, whom you mistook for the gardener, has just said your name: "Mary"; in that moment your eyes are opened, you know the risen Christ for who he is, and you want to grab him and never let go. Now say what Western Christians usually say to celebrate that day: "Happy Easter."

If I'm not mistaken, that high-pitched whistle you hear is a little bit of air escaping from the celebratory bladder. It sounds as if no other word were available, so we borrowed one from "Happy Birthday," which has been pretty well trampled by now.

We have no such trouble expressing ourselves at Christmas. "M-e-r-r-r-y Christmas!" comes from the belly and stretches out like an arm and a beer stein. There's joy and release in it, for believers and nonbelievers alike, the sort of joy one might expect to see more of at Easter. New Year's revelers fling out all their feelings in the cry "Happy New Year!" Now, there's a "happy" that means more than happy. It means both "We made it!" and "Let's do it again!" It's a rallying cry from the blood. "Happy Easter," in contrast, seems to be said mostly with the face.

What's wrong? Can't Christians feel the whole joy of Easter? Do words fail them on that best of days?

Maybe so. And maybe words should fail in the face of a mystery as profound as the resurrection. But maybe, too, Christians are inwardly checked by an unexpressed ambivalence toward Easter. Not toward that first, unadulterated event that fills visionary memory, but toward the holiday that history has concocted for us. Easter Sunday is, after all, a parasite that originally infiltrated its host, then outgrew it from within. The host was an ancient Saxon festival in honor of Eastre, pagan goddess of spring and of fertility. (*Eastre* stems from the ancient word *aus,* meaning "dawn," which gave us the Latin *aurora,* our word *east* and place names like *Oostburg,* Wisconsin.) When missionaries brought Christianity to the Saxons in the second century A.D. they were no fools. To avoid persecution, they disguised their new religious rites in local habit. Conveniently, the resurrection of Christ coincided with the festival to Eastre at the start of spring. In A.D. 325 the Council of Nicaea, under Constantine, declared that thereafter the Christian "Easter" should be celebrated on the first Sunday after the first full moon on or after the vernal equinox.

By that time, the parasite had triumphed over the host. Nobody worships Eastre anymore. Yet even today the church's celebration remains on its ancient astrological schedule, bearing the name of a dawn-goddess. The goddess Eastre's terrestrial symbol, the hare, probably grabs more attention than Christ when he visits today's children in the guise of the Easter Bunny.

These ancient minglings have been secured through the ages by the host of analogies that Christians have conveniently appropriated: birth and resurrection, the egg and the tomb, dawn light and the splendor of the transfigured body, the Queen and the Prince, the sun and the Son. And so that tired old pun "Easter Sonrise Service" lives on.

Face it: we've inherited a muddle, and every time the words "Happy Easter" are spoken, we're reminded of it. Modern Christians, especially the commercial variety who buy colored eggs and baskets and plastic grass for their squealing youngsters, don't know who owns Easter, Christ or the Easter Bunny, any more than they know who owns Christmas, Santa Claus or the Baby Jesus. It's hard to say "Happy Easter" without feeling somewhat neutralized by the ambiguities.

Yet there may be another reason people say "Happy Easter" without the spirit of revelry that marks other holidays. This one reflects not the ambiguities of tradition but, instead, a certain clarity of perception about the real significance of Christ's resurrection.

The Christian Easter is not really about fertility and new birth. It's about spiritual triumph and "second birth." It's not a romantic *dream* of the sort that practically everyone makes out of Christmas, but an *awakening* into an enormous supernatural reality.

Easter, then, invites no toasts and high-fives. When radical new understandings dawn, the light that spreads out bears joy. But when reawakenings come, the light that floods in brings peace.

# God Has
# a Wonderful Plan
# for Your Life

I n the fall of 1969, a strange thing happened to the students at the Christian high schools in western Michigan. They got religion! As if pot, Nixon, Vietnam and *Sgt. Pepper's Lonely Hearts Club Band* weren't unsettling enough, the region was invaded by Bill Bright's Campus Crusade for Christ. The Campus Crusaders infiltrated shopping malls, schools and suburban neighborhoods, stopping the unwary with the unsettling question: "Did you know that God loves you and has a wonderful plan for your life?" They waved little booklets of "Four Spiritual Laws," a kind of shrinky-dink version of Christian theology which took dead aim at the listener's heart. Who is on the "throne" in your life, they asked, your self or Jesus? They offered simple line drawings, proof texts about God's plan of salvation and a short prayer that referred to the conversion of the listener's heart as a done deal.

"Pray this prayer right now," the booklet said, "and Christ will come into your life." Presto.

As they went around performing sidewalk heart surgery, they inspired mass queasiness among believers and unbelievers alike, but for the alienated children of the churched, who filled the Christian high schools of western Michigan, they offered a very appealing prospect: truth without religion. Without organized religion, that is. For a small price—an embarrassing and possibly tear-washed confession in the presence of a stranger—one could have eternal life *and* membership in a spiritual peace generation, a generation less conformist and materialistic than the Pepsi generation, more transient and idealistic than the hippies. No incense, no catechisms, no offerings. No bulletins, litanies, tithing, consistories or white shirts and ties. Just hot, in-your-face, right now, on-your-knees truth. Here and there a person accepted Campus Crusade's plan for his or her life. It was so square it was radical.

All of that was in the air when a team of Campus Crusade weightlifters came to town. At our high-school assembly, they spent about twenty minutes doing four-hundred-pound squats and Olympic-level clean and jerks; then, with pectorals still quivering, each stepped up to the microphone and delivered a direct, heart-squeezing testimony about how he had come to give his life to the Lord. To a crowd of a thousand overly catechized and jaded young churchgoers like myself, this was unprecedented candor.

Not long after the weightlifters completed the local Christian-high-school assembly circuit, a team of student leaders from a sister high school was sent over to lead a routine exchange chapel. We expected the usual twaddle: a future seminarian would open with prayer, an organ virtuoso would lead in lackluster singing, a group of nerds would sing a quartet and the blond class president and president of the varsity club would smile his way through a speech about "running the good race." We got, instead, a shock that is still reverberating in the lives of those who were there.

With raw courage modeled after that of the weightlifters, the visiting student leaders dispensed with formalities and simply told their captive audience what Christ, in person, had done in their hearts.

Then they turned the microphone over to members of the audience, inviting them to come on stage and share their own testimonies. The silence in the auditorium raged like a wild boar. But, at last, a girl not known for her chastity, shall we say, slunk up the center aisle and accepted the mike. With her raccoon mascara running, she sobbed that she had always been messed up but begged us all to take a chance on her now. She felt completely broken and ready to start out clean. She was feeling God's forgiveness in her life right there and then, she said, and wanted us to forgive her and show patience with her struggle to lead an obedient life.

After that stunner came the deluge. Two came up. Then five. Then dozens more, including me. And before long the auditorium stage was S.R.O., jammed with students huddling, jabbering, crying, praying. The seats in the auditorium had emptied of all but a few supine holdouts.

The school was shut down that day. The principal and teachers tried to herd students back to their classes, but their voices were drowned in the roar. Teachers who stormed the hallways trying to break up rings of praying hooligans found brotherly and sisterly arms wrapped about their shoulders and were sucked into prayer. A force more powerful than class rank, sports stardom, sex appeal or SATs was sweeping the building. This wasn't church. It wasn't school. It was faith on fire. Rumor went around that the Holy Spirit had arrived.

God has a wonderful plan for your life, the weightlifters had said. The phrase had disturbed me then, and even as I was joining in the mass conversion, it disturbed me still. At first I had winced at the word *wonderful*. It was one of those "utility words" we had been warned about in English class, like *nice, terrific* and *awful*. It could mean anything the speaker meant to imply, and so it meant nothing. As gum-snapping teenagers, we knew that nothing in this life was exactly full of wonder. Life was full of wonderful expectations and miserable little disappointments. Wonder was for stupid kids.

The idea of a *plan* was disturbing, too. The draft board had a "plan" for people's lives. So did the John Birch Society and the Mormons at the front door. Seventeen was old enough to know that whenever anybody had a "plan" for your life, you were apt to start losing important things like freedom, sanity and your wallet. On the whole, "God has a wonderful plan for your life" had sounded like organization talk—smiley, sanitized, impersonal, like "Have a nice day." It smelled of blueprints and growth projections and perhaps faintly of lotus.

And yet here I was, swept up in all the excitement, touched as never before by a sense that God was poking me in the chest. I had scoffed at little booklets showing a cross on a throne, with an S for "self" at the foot of the throne like the king's Pomeranian. And yet I, along with hundreds of others, was now going through a remarkable ego-thrashing and, in accordance with the wisdom of the new movement, was asking of each event, "What would Christ do?" I may have scorned the Campus Crusade diagram, but in my own way, I suppose, I was living it.

Such was the spirit of those winged-out times that this feeling of liberation from rules but obedience to God quickly came to be referred to as "naturally stoned." I can only hint at how exciting it was. But being naturally stoned seemed to be equal parts order and disorder, plan and no plan. Many of us had jumped from a carousel onto the back of a real horse, a rearing stallion, but had no idea how to steer it. Was this God's plan—this school-stopping anarchy?

Two days after the wave of spiritual fervor swept our high school, I found myself at the front of a school assembly trying to help sort out my own and everyone else's confusion. A lot of disorder and reordering was happening in our midst, I told the still-buzzing crowd. A certain amount of it showed proof of genuine soul-searching and the Holy Spirit's guidance, and a certain amount was probably an emotional spasm that would soon pass. "Test the spirits," I warned. "God's plan for our lives cannot be boiled down into 'four spiritual laws.' We could all put a cross on the throne in our hearts, right now, but would our lives beyond that point breed more love or more spite?" The fruit of the Spirit, I said, quoting Galatians 5:22, is "love, joy, peace, patience, kindness, goodness, faithfulness, gentleness and self-control." By their fruits you will know them.

The irony of my cautionary speech was that it soon landed me a job as our school's spokesman in an exchange chapel at a Christian high school in Kalamazoo. Yes, we offered our personal testimonies. No, I did not use the phrase "God has a wonderful plan for your life." Yes, I invited people to come out of the bleachers and seize the mike. No, I wasn't exactly sure of what I was doing. I remember feeling that as emcee I had the safest job in the house. I knew what was going to happen.

Yes, we stopped their school that day. Bleachers emptying toward the stage, clusters of praying converts, hallways choked, teachers full of joy and consternation. This amazing upheaval was beginning to appear to be the plan. There was no stopping it. Whole regions were getting naturally stoned. We might go national.

But out of all the uproar at the high school in Kalamazoo, I have preserved one special memory that has helped me keep a stabilizing perspective over the years. While all the hullabaloo was still under way, I remember standing by the doorway of an abandoned classroom confronting three particularly intelligent, hairy and vocal students. One was the editor of the school newspaper. Another was the president of its student body. Another was their friend. Their breath smelled of smoke, and they were happy to blow it in my face, along with their cynical view of the sheep who were bleating all around us.

In their own intellectual manner, they had been trying to disrupt the school, had played pranks and played devil's advocate in the student paper. They saw the larger horizon of marches on Washington, civil-rights struggles, the Vietnam War, the revolution in rock and roll, the hypocrisies of their comfortable middle-class elders. They wanted to see their world turned inside out, but not in this way. Not with altar calls and mass hysteria. Not with Christianity, plain or fancy. They were agnostics at best. And because I had been the emcee, I was the one they wanted to debate.

I admit it: they trashed me. They were sharp, well-read, mentally adroit and hot for a fight. I was simple, confessional, bemused by ironies. We argued circles around each other. It was three against one.

Who knows who made what impression on whom that day? All I know is that within the next couple of years, the president of the student body killed himself. The third friend became a genial, well-read, quiet and still cynical employee of a typesetter. The newspaper editor took his dangling greasy black locks to a Christian college, where he became for a while a prominent atheist and prize-winning poet. After college—trust me on this—he became an Episcopal priest.

And here I am, writing this book.

God has a wonderful plan for your life, all right. And it's wild.

# D.V.

Why, you do not even know what will happen tomorrow. What is your life?
You are a mist that appears for a little while and then vanishes. Instead,
you ought to say, "If it is the Lord's will, we will live and do this or that."

JAMES 4:14-15

N early extinct, as rare as a blue-footed booby, is the abbreviation "D.V.," short for the Latin phrase *Deo volente,* which means "God willing." It won't be spotted in the overgrazed flatlands of everyday conversation. But when I was growing up it made a showy appearance from time to time in the devotional rhetoric of denominational periodicals. When I moved to northwest Iowa to teach at a small Christian college, "D.V." appeared again in the speech of some young people, especially the offspring of Canadian Dutch immigrants. According to a sarcastic few, "D.V." was an abbreviation for a Dutch phrase, "De Lord Villing."

The phrase will roost nervously anywhere in the syntactic branches of a sentence:

☐ D.V., the reunion will take place at six o'clock on July 23rd.

☐ He vowed that, D.V., he would dedicate the rest of his career to the Chicago urban ministry.

☐ [poster] . . . will meet at the Lutheran Camp on Lake Okoboji,

D.V. and weather permitting.

Whenever I hear or see the phrase, I fix on it with a kind of fascination-repulsion, without exactly knowing why. To unfamiliar eyes, it may look like nonsense, a printer's error. And it usually strikes me as unfamiliar until my mind catches up with my eye. Then I recognize it as a code phrase, linking me to all the others who hold the key.

Who are those keyholders? Are they plainly the sanctified, who defer to God's will in all their ways? Or, at the other extreme, are they an ethnic or denominational in-group using jaded language forms to fortify, encircle and protect their privileges? No easy answers. The two families mingle and marry, often in the same individual—I should know.

I'm impressed by the phrase's ancient and universal provenance. Gideon was saying "God willing" when he laid out the fleece. Wherever people have slaughtered lambs, burned incense, divined entrails, read tea leaves, danced for rain or said grace before lunch, they have made their concessions to the will of God or the gods. My Muslim friends drop "God willing" into their conversations without skipping a beat. Some of my Catholic friends do the same.

It appears to be a human impulse, by no means confined to Christianity, to duck a little when stating plans for the future. Having seen tornadoes, tuberculosis, earthquakes, plagues of locust and broken bones, humankind knows better than to say, unequivocally, "I will" or "It will." There has always been that unpredictable element—the turn of fortune's wheel, gremlins, "acts of God," a benign providence, Wyrd or the caprice of a jealous Yahweh—to consider and, perhaps, appease.

The ancient Maya ritually excised the hearts of living prisoners. Most of our attempts to appease the powers are less dramatic. We throw a pinch of salt over the shoulder. We say, "With luck, we should be there by nightfall." We say, "Knock on wood," as we knock on wood. We say, "Keep your fingers crossed," as we implement the best-laid plans of mice and men—like launching a space shuttle with flawed O-rings. And, in certain circles, we say "D.V.," with not much different inflections. I'd call them word offerings, tributes to the Almighty, just in case he's there, or to anything else in the universe that might serve the same function.

In most of these cases, the meaning has little to do with any outwardly referential sense of the words. It may hardly matter to us, as we speak, whether the concept of "luck" is anything more than a benign delusion or whether crossing the fingers *really* speeds the wish on its way. (Revealingly, we make the same gesture behind our backs when we want to lie and get away with it.) Similarly, one may say "D.V." without being the least interested in discerning God's will. What counts for meaning, instead, is the gesture of breaking midsentence, creating a verbal absence to mark a spot where we acknowledge the finiteness of our control. With such a gesture we cut a little hole in the thatched roof of human certitude so that the smoke of our fatedness can escape.

For creating verbal absences, or empty verbalisms, it is convenient to use a form of language like "D.V." that is three times removed from sense. As an abbreviation it serves simply as an index to a word, opaque in itself. Furthermore, it's an abbreviation of a forgotten phrase, or more aptly, a phrase not forgotten because, in most cases, it was never learned. And, finally, it's an abbreviation of a forgotten phrase in a "dead" language. How many people recall, except hazily, that

|  | stands for the Latin | which means |
|---|---|---|
| e.g. | *exempli gratia* | for example |
| etc. | *et cetera* | and other things |
| i.e. | *id est* | that is |

D.V., though not worn quite as smooth from handling, ranks among these. Though most of us have forgotten what they mean, we know the slots in which to drop them. They're the linguistic equivalents of bus tokens.

And that's what bothers me. Why should the honorable English phrase "God willing" be avoided while a cryptic little slug of an

expression like "D.V." is preferred? To some Protestant ears, if I am
not mistaken, phrases with the word "God" in them, like "for God's
sake," "God only knows" or "God willing," sound faintly like swearing (though *"Lord* willing" falls easily from these folks' tongues).
Some will leave "God willing" to their unbelieving neighbors while
adopting a phrase like "D.V.," which sounds clean, efficient, even a
little jaunty.

Personally, I'm not so short on time that I need the abbreviation,
any more than I need the X in *Xmas.* I don't need expressions that
invoke the name of God in one breath and in the same breath efface
it. And I don't need Christian code words any more than I need my
old Sunday-school pins.

Whether one says "God willing" in English, Latin, or Serbo-Croa-
tian, however, the question pressing upon the human race is not
whether the correct phrase has been employed or whether proper
deference has been paid to the real powers that govern human destiny. Jesus told his disciples in his sermon on the mountain: "Not
everyone who says to me, 'Lord, Lord,' will enter the kingdom of
heaven, but only he who does the will of my Father who is in heav-
en" (Mt 7:21). "Do" is the command and "the will of my Father" is
the norm. Merely acknowledging that will and allowing for its impact
is not at all the same thing as loving it, understanding it and doing
it. Not by 180.

The history of the ancient Israelites is a story of their continual—
pardon the cliché—talking the talk but not walking the walk. "You
have forgotten God your Savior," charged Isaiah; "you have not re-
membered the Rock, your fortress" (Is 17:10). About a hundred years
later, shortly before the fall of Jerusalem to Nebuchadnezzar in 587
B.C., Jeremiah was repeating the charge: "Does a maiden forget her
jewelry, a bride her wedding ornaments? Yet my people have forgotten me, days without number" (Jer 2:32). Because it forgot the main
point, Israel suffered unspeakable grief. As far as I can tell, the rest
of us have little reason to gloat.

That history of wandering and betrayal gives tremendous resonance, tremendous poignancy, to the moment of Christ's vigil in the Garden of Gethsemane when he confessed to his disciples that his soul was "overwhelmed with sorrow to the point of death" (Mt 26:38). In a moment he personally rectified that whole national-historical-theological muddle, the moment when, earnestly wishing to be spared the coming pain, he prayed to the Father, "Yet not as I will, but as you will" (Mt 26:39). And then he went out and did it— D.V., or however you want to phrase it.

If that scene doesn't in some depth of our spirit come to mind when we use "D.V.," we might as well ditch the phrase.

# God Told Me

I n San Dimas, California, where Bill and Ted of movie fame began their "excellent adventure," lives a different sort of adventurer named Bob Haifley. According to the *Los Angeles Times,* Mr. Haifley spent five years, 2,500 work-hours and a lot of glue building a life-sized figure of the crucified Christ out of 65,000 toothpicks. It hangs from a wire in his garage against a black background, illuminated by a spotlight, looking so impressively lifelike that a sixteen-year-old neighbor could only say "Whoa!"

Bill and Ted undertook their movie journey under the guidance of a shades-wearing alien from the future named Rufus. What made Haifley, a humble water-department supervisor and nonartist, start collecting toothpicks and inviting the ridicule of his neighbors by building San Dimas's answer to Noah's Ark?

"God told me to do it," he says.

According to Haifley, God not only commissioned the work one day as Haifley drove his pickup truck through San Dimas, but showed him how to do the spiky hair and crown of thorns after five years of indecision. God even gave him a title for the piece: *The Gift.*

Haifley would make a good candidate for straitjacket tester at a local brain laundry, you might think, except that his bright eyes and uplifted smile make him look like the sort of man you'd want for your child's soccer coach. And the Toothpick Christ is doing no harm, hanging there in bristling serenity. Haifley says he believes God is using him to inspire people.

Could it be that God Almighty, Maker of heaven and earth, really told him to do it?

Such a claim has been made before. There was Noah, of course, and Jonah—we know what happened to him when he refused to listen. There were the Samuels and Nathans and Jeremiahs. There was the apostle Paul and the emperor Constantine the Great, who, according to Eusebius, saw a cross in the sky at the battle of Mulvian Bridge and under it the words *In hoc signo vincere* (in this sign conquer). If God could have spoken to such as these, could he not speak to someone like Bob Haifley?

On the other hand, if he was speaking directly to the Toothpick Man, how about all the fire-starters, the wing-walkers, the tower-sitters, the cave-dwellers, the televangelists, the Christian skinheads, the ayatollahs, the Ku Kluxers, the abortion-clinic bombers, the Jim Joneses, the Son of Sams, the baby beaters and the necrophiliacs who calmly tell reporters that God told them to do it? Do they all have direct hookups?

And what about the financially struggling young mother who says, "While I was deep in prayer, God told me, as clear as I'm talking to you, that my strength was not sufficient but he would see me through"? What about the Spirit-stoked Christian rock musician who says, "God gave me these lyrics the day I laid off acid"? What about the missionary-minded young person who stands up in church, saying, "I prayed all last week that God would make clear to me whether I should go to Turkey, despite my conservative Chinese parents' opposition, and I have a strong sense now that God is telling me I should go. He told me to have faith in him, that the money for my support would come from God's people, and that eventually I would make my parents proud"? What voices are they hearing that the average pew-fillers do not? What do they mean when they say, "God told me"?

A little caution is in order. If God speaks to me, as clearly as I'm speaking to you, his voice must have to carry above the din in that vast auditorium in my mind and body where hour after hour the sloppy rehearsals of daily life go on. I can make out some of the competing voices in there. The bowels speak of last night's Hawaiian pizza. My fifth-grade teacher says, "You have such talent, but you're wasting it with your naughtiness." My dead grandpa reads aloud from a toastmaster's book, preaches sermons, prays at dinner, jousts with Einstein, praises Paul Tournier. I hear old saws: A bird in the hand is worth two in the bush. He who laughs, lasts. The scriptwriting team in my brain coaches me: "You should have said, 'OK, it's over.' That's what you should have said." The lookout in my brain puts the binoculars down and says, "If that ever happens again, stay cool. Don't hyperventilate." My desires say, "Get some more. Now. Not that one, the other one. Wow." The monitor in me says, "You're mellowing." Guilt says, "What if they find out?" My "inner parents" say, "Check all the angles before you make a move." My inner child says, "That's mine and I want it." My inner tape says, "You don't deserve it." Friends beckon through the din: "You never write!" My eyes send me warnings: "Watch the overhang." "Merging traffic." TV jingles drone on: "I can't believe I ate the whole thing." "Feel the heartbeat of America." Headlines, rules, catechism lessons, psychobabble, radio call-letters, molecules on my eardrums, the devil on one shoulder and the angel on the other, the music of the spheres and the savage rumblings of monsters of the deep. Voices, voices, voices.

If God should step into that cavernous, cacophonous rehearsal hall and calmly say, "I want you to make a toothpick Christ," what are the chances I would hear him? Even hearing him, what are the chances I would recognize the voice as his and not think it another government report concerning that Hawaiian pizza? I don't have an answer. It could be that the whole rabble of false, familiar voices would make a perfect foil for that distinctive new one, a voice so pure, intense and intimate, so resonant, so right for me, so unmistakably a "word of knowledge" that it could have come only from God.

But more caution is in order. Even if I vow that "God told me" and I don't care what anybody says, how are you to know what that means? I might be reporting any of the following:

□ I saw a heavenly messenger in glorious raiment and heard his words.

□ I heard clear words that seemed to come from God.

□ God spoke to me in a dream.

□ I felt a strong compulsion that I believe to be from God.

□ I felt a strange pressure from somewhere outside of me.

□ I think I knew what God would want me to do.

□ I couldn't resist.

□ I wanted.

There is room in that list for everyone from Jonah to Jim Jones.

But when I'm through being cautious, acting the role of the spiritual CPA, I'm not really content. I see that glint of well-being in Bob Haifley's eye. I feel the cathedral-like sanctity in the dark of his garage. And it's impossible for me not to be impressed by the magnificent triviality of the spiritual adventure he has embarked upon, the portion of wisdom in his foolishness.

I don't want to live in a world where, as a rule, no God can speak through the hearts and minds of his creatures. I don't want to live in a world where truth and sanity are measured by suburbia's crushed velvet and barbecue tongs. I want to suppose that God could speak to me, when I get close to him, as well as to any other. And would it be foolish to believe that a God who made heaven and earth could also make himself heard through a radio deejay, an old saw, a memory of my grandpa or even those rumblings from Hawaii?

But what if everyone walked around saying God told me this and God told me that? Who could be believed?

I don't know if that's any more of a problem than it's ever been. As Christ said, "By their fruit you will recognize them. . . . Every good tree bears good fruit, but a bad tree bears bad fruit" (Mt 7:16-17). And the fruit of the Spirit is unmistakable, as Paul told the Galatians: it's love, joy, peace, patience, kindness, goodness, faithfulness, gentleness and self-control (Gal 5:22-23). If the wisdom really comes from God, according to James, it will be "first of all pure; then peace-loving, considerate, submissive, full of mercy and good fruit, impartial and sincere" (Jas 3:17).

Somewhere in there, I think I can find room for Bob Haifley's "excellent adventure."

# Unequally Yoked

B ug zappers are those ghostly blue things you see humming in some people's yards at night. They're usually posted toward the edge of a property, their job being to electrocute potential pests before they cross over into the living space. Maybe you've seen them crackling merrily in the gloom, every spark an epitaph.

The nearest thing to a verbal bug zapper that I know of is the phrase "unequally yoked," the way I heard it used when I was growing up.

"Unequally yoked" draws its electricity from the words of the apostle Paul in 2 Corinthians 6:14, where he warned the new Christians at Corinth against being mismatched with unbelievers. The Greek word he used—*heterozygountes*—was based on the word *zygos*, which could mean either a yoke, as in the brace connecting a pair of oxen ahead of a wagon, or the beam connecting the two sides of a balance scale. A beam and a yoke look somewhat alike and serve similar purposes. Both unite what ought to be equal sides: equal in power or equal in weight. Christians have always had a hard time learning precisely what it means to be *in* but not *of* the world. That's a vital but difficult balance, and the Corinthians, apparently, were leaning a little too much toward *of.*

Paul's warning against unholy alliances must have fried a few business deals and estranged a few bedfellows. It seemed to cover the whole scope of Christian life. But he was building an electrified fence to deal with fairly large game. Somewhere in the two thousand years it took for "unequally yoked" to get to me, the game got smaller and smaller and smaller.

First, "yoked" came to refer almost exclusively to marriage, the most radical of partnerships. "Unequally yoked" came to mean "marrying outside the faith." To a Protestant child in the 1950s that would mean, Don't marry an unbeliever. Don't marry a Jew. Don't marry a Catholic. There will be unending conflicts. You'll both stop going to church. Worse yet, you may convert to keep the peace. What will become of the children? Will they be baptized or bar mitzvahed? You'll break your mother's heart. In short, it's a bad idea. Don't do it.

Most of the popular warnings against marrying far outside one's faith can, I imagine, be empirically shown to be sound advice. Many people, in the fever of love and courtship, underestimate the hold of their ancestral religion upon them. Some try to bury it, for the sake of harmony with a mate, but like a Cockney accent or a sunken boat, it tends after a few storms to reemerge, outlines intact. Where each parent clings to his or her own faith, that faith is as much in danger of becoming privatized as of becoming relativized. Children do tend to grow confused in interfaith households, though some are broadened as well. Where there is marital strain within an interfaith household, the greatest danger is that a child's religious rearing may become the field where parental power-plays unfold. In such cases, the parents' spiritual dysfunction can be as damaging as sexual dysfunction in its effects upon a child's psychosocial development.

But parents in my experience were after smaller game. As I was growing up in the Dutch Christian Reformed community in Grand Rapids, wearing a denominational straitjacket so slim and so tight it was indistinguishable from my skin, the fear of Catholicism and other faiths had been so deeply inculcated in me—the word *inculcate* is appropriate because it comes from Latin words that literally mean to trample into with one's heel—that I did not need to be warned against intermarriage. Holy water, limbo, St. Christopher on the dashboard; the pope, for Pete's sake! The imagination of it made me nauseous.

The real threat to all was that I, being Christian Reformed, might become interested in a little girl from the Reformed Church of America (RCA). We believed in supporting a system of Christian schools. They didn't. Beyond that, we were separated by different patterns of immigration and assimilation, different accents on philosophy and doctrine, and historically scattered incidents of personal intolerance that stuck in people's craws. Our denominations supported rival colleges. The rest of our differences would have been undetectable to an audience of average Americans at twenty paces. I could see no harm in marrying across that line, and perhaps my own parents didn't either, but I believe the imagination of it made some of my elders nauseous.

In their fear, they would ignore the bird of marriage and set traps for the flies of curiosity and the mosquitoes of desire.

"Mom, I kinda like that DeVries girl."

"Is she one of ours?"

"She's RCA, I think."

"Hm. Be careful, son.

"I'm not talking about marrying her, Mom."

"Just bear in mind what Paul says about being unequally yoked."

ZZZZAAAAPPPP! There in the moist night air another tiny life is lost, and the burnt hulls gather like popcorn debris in the bottom of a bowl.

The feisty woman I married in 1978 came from an even smaller, more uptight and more doctrine-proud denomination than my own. It shall remain nameless.

Not a word of disapproval was voiced at our wedding. But the laugher, for me, was to learn later that her mom had warned her all her life against becoming "unequally yoked" with such a one as I.

The mosquitoes of desire may have gotten zapped, but it looks as if the bird of marriage found a roost.

# God Wants You to Succeed

*P*sst! You, with the maxed-out credit cards. You, watching the odometer turn over on your car. You, reaching for the generic saltines. Aren't you sick of scraping along? Aren't you about ready for some slicker threads, like on that dude stepping out of the BMW? Aren't you ready for the "abundant" life? I'm talking gold fixtures, croissants, straighter teeth, box seats, designer labels for the kids, crackerjack legal help and bucks left over for the paralyzed vets. I'm talking Cancun, man. Club Med. I'm talking tax shelters, private schools. Wouldn't you like to be disease-free? And on top of that, how about a closer walk with God?

I've got news for you, pal: God wants you to succeed. He's a powerful God, more powerful than you've ever imagined. He can do anything, change anything, heal anything, make anything happen. He's fabulous, man.

And the best part? He's all yours. That's right. He's made himself available to you. Without restriction.

No, no. I don't mean he's politely standing by with a table full of gift items hoping you might pray for a few. He gives gifts, but those are negligible compared to what I'm talking about. And I don't mean he's up there in heaven rooting for you to get saved, though he does want you to be saved: that's the ultimate definition of "success." I'm not even focusing on that stuff about Jesus' dying and rising again, succeeding in his war against the devil so you can have eternal life in him. I'm not talking about what's in him. I'm talking about what's in you.

Come closer. What I'm talking about is a secret so deep you can't get no deeper. If you grew up in one of those orthodox churches—you know, those big dead ones downtown—they probably didn't dare give you this in Sunday school. They were probably afraid if the whole church got the message, it might wake up and start kicking butt, religiously speaking—and they didn't want that to happen. But I'm going to let you have it, free of charge. Right now. Here it is: God is a spiritual principle in you. Do you hear me? He's the spiritual power that created the world and makes everything happen in it. That same power is in you, whether you believe it yet or not. The whole material world is just an illusion, a crust over the spiritual power that runs it. Now, you can let yourself be poor and sick, the victim of chance events on the material plane. Or you can claim that spiritual power inside and claim the health and wealth that's coming to you.

Don't worry about whether it will work or not. It works. God made the spiritual laws that run the universe—you don't think he'd violate his own laws, do you? He can't. If he did, he wouldn't be God. That's what I meant when I said he's available to you without restriction. Use him the way he wants you to use him.

You see, the spiritual plane is all one fabric. When you shake one corner of a blanket, the other side ripples. So don't just *beg* God for necessities and healing from all your ridiculous and completely un-necessary little diseases. *Shake* the blanket. Have faith! Believe that you already *have* whatever you want—blooming good health, a hap-py family, a promotion, a European vacation—and those things on the purely material plane will be coming your way, rolling in, ruled by the spirit, *your* spirit, the spirit of God! Don't admit to being sick or poor. That sends out negative vibrations, dragging you and everybody down. All you have to do to get the success you want is to name it and claim it.

Name it and claim it. Catchy, huh? And true!

Now if you see somebody groaning over some blood disease or lining up dejected at a soup kitchen, you can be pretty sure that person hasn't learned the secret of God's power. Hasn't learned to be successful, in God's sense of the word. Of course, if you get sick or have a short-term financial setback—what we call a cash flow problem—forget about it. Keep your eyes on the prize. Your bodily success may not have arrived, yet, but it's coming. It's coming. Rolling in on the wave of your belief. Negative thinking *is* sickness. Negative thinking *is* poverty. But faith in God is success already.

God wants you to succeed. If you're not succeeding, you have nobody to blame but yourself. Are you the type that wants proof texts? OK, I've got one for you—Mark 11:22-24:

> "Have faith in God," Jesus answered. "I tell you the truth, if anyone says to this mountain, 'Go, throw yourself into the sea,' and does not doubt in his heart but believes that what he says will happen, it will be done for him. Therefore I tell you, whatever you ask for in prayer, believe that you have received it, and it will be yours."

Some of these sad-sack theology professors like to come back at me with verses of their own. Like Philippians 4:12:

> I know what it is to be in need, and I know what it is to have plenty. I have learned the secret of being content in any and every situation, whether well fed or hungry, whether living in plenty or in want. I can do everything through him who gives me strength.

Or 1 Timothy 6:6: "But godliness with contentment is great gain."

My answer to the professor is, What kind of salary are you pulling, buddy? If you can do everything, why are you driving that '78 Buick LeSabre? Why are your teenage kids still sharing a bedroom in your tiny house? I don't see much receiving, so I'd guess there's not much believing. I like to see these stuttering professors try to wiggle around Mark 11:24. As far as I'm concerned, that's the main point in the Bible. Heck, that's about the only point I need. That one throws the door open wide.

Come a little closer here. I don't want us to be overheard. I see you flipping through that little booklet *The Prosperity Gospel* by Charles Hummel. Don't waste your time. I'll tell you what it says. I read it, and I'm not threatened. It says that prosperity theology grew out of the Faith Movement in the 1970s, started by Kenneth Hagin. OK? It says he had picked up some ideas from the Pentecostal movement, faith healing from around the turn of the century, and some New Thought from a guy called Essek William Kenyon—the same metaphysical stuff that went into Christian Scientism, Unity and Divine Science. From Hagin it went on through radio and TV preachers like Kenneth and Gloria Copeland, Jerry Savelle, Frederick Price, Bob Tilton and Oral Roberts. It could have added Rev. Ike and Robert Schuller. Anyway, your booklet says that prosperity theology has a "dualistic" worldview and that our doctrines of human nature, Christ's atonement and the deification of the Christian are "major deviations" from historic Christianity.

He's entitled to his opinion. We're always getting hit with criticism. Some people say we're reviving the gnostic heresy—you know, flesh/ spirit dualism and the claim to direct perception of divine truth, over and above faith? I have to laugh. I don't like being called a heretic, but maybe the Gnostics should get more credit.

Some people say we're just trying to make people spiritually comfortable with the materialism of the Western world. I wouldn't say "comfortable." I'd say *ambitious*—ambitious to reach all the success God has planned for us. Spiritual and material success. Both. But first of all spiritual. If that's materialism and narcissism, I say give me more of it. We're still trying to yank people out of their Puritan blues. We've got to break them out of their guilt and gloom, their self-denying, penitential, tail-dragging, finger-wagging funk. These people need to be turned inside out! Lit up by the spirit! Instead of saying no all the time, they need to say yes to the possibilities of creation. They need to say, "Please, Sir, I want some more" to the Guy who dishes up the porridge.

This English professor came over once and told me that the sentence "God wants you to succeed" is a "pseudostatement." "It purports to be a declarative statement grounded in observation or experience," he said, "but it's nothing more than a stock utterance, devoid of content. It's a slogan." I laughed at the poor bespectacled man and said, "I grant it's a slogan. But it's a successful one, don't you agree?"

And then there was a lady who thought prosperity theology was New Age religion under a thin covering of Christianity. I told her to stick in Jesus for crystals and find some support in the Bible and maybe we could talk. Turned out she wasn't for New Age but against it. I think she was ready to throw out prosperity theology with the bath water.

All the criticism just proves to me we're doing the right thing. Christ said his followers would be persecuted, and we are. So I'm not worried. Thanks to radio and TV, we're growing. We're moving. People in practically every church accept the prosperity doctrine in one form or another. People believe it when times are tough. They also believe it when the stock market's on a roll. You won't find many who object to the idea that God wants us to succeed. That's like objecting to the idea that God wants us to breathe.

I know you've got to go, but before you do, may I share a little something with you? It's another very important passage, Mark 10:29-30. Jesus says, and I paraphrase: if you give everything you've got to me and the gospel, then, in this present life, you'll receive one hundred times as much in return. You can read the verses around it in your spare time. But do you hear the message? It's the secret to success that every prosperous Christian knows: in order to receive, you've got to give, but giving to God is the best investment you can make. One-hundredfold!

Now if you're looking for a way to give to God, may I suggest a donation to our Word of Ambition television ministry? Give till your pockets are empty, and God will crown your generosity with success. We'll accept checks, money orders, VISA, MasterCard or American Express. We also take pledges and will send out monthly reminders for periodic payments.

Remember: God wants you to succeed. Just name it and claim it. And if you're looking for an opening, some ministry you can call your own, consider television. We're talking some serious bucks.

# There Must Be a Reason

Sure there's a reason. Ronald blew his job interview because he was worrying about his palms and his armpits. And he was sweating like melted swiss because he felt so ill-dressed. He felt ill-dressed because he was wearing an eight-year-old corduroy sport coat and a clown tie left over from the sixties. He wore his old duds because all his clothes money had gone into a new carburetor. The money had gone into parts for the old Honda because he and his wife hadn't saved up for a down payment on a new car. Their savings came up double zeroes because they had been scrambling to pay off credit card debt. The debts were lapping at the ceiling because when these two were young marrieds they had made only minimum loan repayments for years. They had outborrowed their income because they'd been impatient to furnish their first several apartments. They were impatient to look prosperous because Georgette—that's Ronald's wife—had been reared in a wealthy home and her father had once jeered at Ronald when Ronald had boasted that he and Georgette could cut it in a trendy apartment complex in Chicago. Ronald had married "up" because he had felt deprived of material possessions as a boy. He had had those feelings because he *had* been deprived—his parents had survived the Great Depression and since then, they had locked up every spare dollar in insurance policies and real estate. In first grade, he had had to eat carrot sticks and blue-boiled eggs for lunch.

So, yes, there are reasons Ronald is now without a job. But these reasons all point back over his shoulder at the trail of choices he has made among the givens of his life. Part nature, part nurture, some would say. That's how the cookie crumbles. He made his bed, now he has to lie in it.

If Ronald's spiritually minded friends thought these were the only reasons that counted, they probably wouldn't say a thing. They'd let the historians, sociologists, psychoanalysts and geneticists close the casebook on Ronald. But they don't.

Instead, Ronald's friend Gloria says, "There must be a reason."

What does she mean?

That's impossible to say exactly, because her phrase is exquisitely imprecise. In a general vapor of compassion for her friend, she implies: there must be a reason, though she doesn't know it. She rejects the idea that Chance rules the world or that her friend Ronald is just a poor, schleppy victim of circumstances. And she doesn't buy the deterministic line that says the whole of Ronald's past environment and genetic makeup account entirely for the fix he's in right now.

What she *does* know, she implies, is that what Ronald is becoming and what is becoming of Ronald are more important than anything Ronald has been or done in the past. In other words, she has hope for Ronald's future.

Gloria's statement, "There must be a reason," is a very broad signal of some kind of faith. But you'd have to know Gloria to have any idea what her faith is in. Her words don't reveal it. Her comment could easily mean, "Ronald picked the wrong day for a job interview. He's a Leo, and Mars is in the House of the Ram, so he should hold off all business contacts until . . ." But she's not an astrologer. Nor is she a New Age pop mystic.

Gloria is a Christian. I'm sure of that because I invented her myself for the sake of this essay. When she says, "There must be a reason," she vaguely has in mind God and God's will, not just for Ronald's life but for the whole creation. She has no idea why God would permit Ronald to crash-land at his job interview, but she believes that the purpose of the entire creation is to reflect glory upon its Maker. Somehow, she believes, God has included Ronald in the working out of a plan that will, in the end, bring fitting praise to God's name.

Now, Gloria has been watching cable TV lately, the religious channel. She's heard some men with white hair and rolled-back eyes say that God wants his people to succeed. They sounded a little too much like insurance salesmen for her, and she thought those quivering jowls looked quite silly under all that angel hair. But she hadn't been thinking about much else in the meantime, so when she said, "There must be a reason," she pretty much assumed the reason was that God had a better job in store for Ronald, if he'd just keep up the job search.

Well, maybe. But even if she is right about God, she might be wrong about the reason. Ronald might need to replace a certain amount of macho pride with a nurturing attitude, time in his socks and housecoat, time among the Lego blocks with his preschool-aged rug rats. Georgette may need a period of work outside the home to discover some of her latent gifts. Ronald might be entering a period of steep decline, ending in depression and suicide. The whole circle of his friends may use his death as an occasion to examine their hearts and rediscover the meaning of life. Or Ronald might be about to read a book in his spare time that will bring him an inspired idea that will flower into a charitable business that will help to mend hundreds of broken lives. Or he might mope around a neighborhood café, reading the want ads, be observed by a young novelist who builds him into a fictional character at the center of a horror novel which is later made into a blockbuster motion picture, which offends the Catholic archbishops and provokes a rare comment on the state of the arts from the pope, which provokes a defensive statement by the current head of the National Endowment for the Arts, which offends Protestant evangelicals, who demonstrate in an unruly fashion outside a nationwide chain of theaters, thus embarrassing an impressionable young man who had meant to go into a seminary but now changes his mind and embarks on a ministry to . . . And so it might go. Reasons lie behind us, but more powerful reasons lie before us.

There must be a reason.

Yes. And God works in mysterious ways.

# Praise the Lord!

P raise is a wonderful thing. For me to praise you or God or anything sincerely I must first be released from my needs, captivated by something's glory and moved to record my response, without any sense that my response is required to improve the thing and without any sense that by offering it I am claiming some of the glory for myself. Genuine praise is thus humble, active, open-hearted, informed, attentive, encouraging and kind. I have a private theory that giving it is in some way necessary to mental health.

To all those who believe in him, the Lord God is wonderful by definition. Wonderful, and worthy to be praised.

"Praise the Lord" should therefore be a wonderful thing to say. For the ancient Israelites it was. Their word *hallelujah*—literally, "praise Yahweh"—and its variations appear more than 150 times in the Old Testament and are echoed in the New. Praising the Lord appears to have topped the Israelites' national agenda. Second Chronicles 20, for

example, tells how Jehoshaphat defeated the armies of Moab and
Ammon without fighting. He simply went forth at the head of his
army and led it in singing the praise of the Lord, whereupon the
invaders weirdly commenced to slaughter one another. Afterwards,
the Israelites praised the Lord some more. For Israel to be Israel, it
had to be obedient, and to be obedient, it had to praise the Lord.

David's language of praise in Psalm 117 turns out to be something
like a prelude to eternity, according to St. John's visionary depiction
of the New Jerusalem:

> The twenty-four elders and the four living creatures fell down and
> worshiped God, who was seated on the throne. And they cried:
>> "Amen, Hallelujah!"
> Then a voice came from the throne, saying:
>> "Praise our God,
>>> all you his servants,
>> you who fear him,
>>> both small and great!"
> Then I heard what sounded like a great multitude, like the roar
> of rushing waters and like loud peals of thunder, shouting:
>> "Hallelujah!
>> For our Lord God Almighty reigns." (Rev 19:4-6)

Not a lot of irony here. This is "Praise the Lord!" or "Hallelujah" at
its best: full-throated, universal and unanimous. Some people react
to good tidings or moments of reprieve by saying "Hallelujah" with
genuine joy. From a solidly Christian perspective, they are momentarily joining the eternal choir, inhabiting heaven under the cloak of
time.

But not everybody who says "Praise the Lord" speaks divinely.
There is a certain conversational style in which the listener wants to
appear to be listening but is giving no thought to what is being said,
has nothing to add and would just as soon be done with the exchange. So he or she keeps repeating the word "Exactly . . . Exactly."
A happier but just as vapid Christian variation on this reply is the
habitual response to all uplifting news with the words "Praise the

Lord." This response has less to do with the heavenly choir than with the earthly herd. It's a kind of contented Christian mooing.

Some who shuttle between secular and Christian groups will work the words "Praise the Lord" into their conversation if they suspect their new counterpart is a Christian. Their use of the phrase as a kind of password and sign of affiliation reminds me of the way some academics spread their suitcoats to let their Phi Beta Kappa keys shine.

In charismatic circles, the accent frequently falls not on the third syllable—"Lord"—but on the first syllable: "Praise." The result is a three-beat metric unit that poets refer to as a dactyl, after the Greek word for finger, an object with three segments: long short short. "*Praise* the Lord." The accent on "praise" starts the whole phrase with a kind of burst, as if the speaker has been at that moment unexpectedly overcome by an impulse welling from within. That impulse to the charismatic is, of course, the very movement of the Holy Ghost, and the words are uttered in such a way that they appear less to have been spoken by the speaker than to have spoken themselves through the speaker, who conceives of him- or herself as an empty vessel, available for use. The impression of helpless submission is often completed by a closing of the eyes, a wagging of the head and a smiling, affectionate "*Thank* you, Jesus."

Who is to say whether this is the form of genuine feeling? It is safe to say, however, that while some people yield to it sincerely, many others find this behavior easy to mimic, and in any fellowship where it becomes established it spreads quickly. Some have feelings that find form; others adopt forms in search of feelings. Some are full of feeling, while others are full of the fear of not feeling. "Praise the Lord" comes from both kinds of lips. And charismatic worship, whose form follows somewhat the pattern of sexual arousal, climax and afterglow, encourages increasing exaggeration in all of its parts. In time, "praise" evolves from a one-syllable word into a two-or-more-syllable word ("pra-a-aise . . ."), and with every added syllable it slips closer to, or deeper into, self-parody.

The straying of more emotionally expressive Christians into self-caricature has not been lost on Hollywood, whose jackals always prey on the weakest of the herd. Hollywood's stereotype of a preacher is a platform-stalking, finger-shaking, quivery-jowled, poofy-haired backwoodsman in a rumpled suit screaming "Pra-aise the Lawd!" Of course, some of the real preachers on cable TV are practically indistinguishable from their celluloid twins. They, too, are whispering, muttering, shouting and sighing—"Praise the Lord!" It's hard to tell who is imitating whom.

That the Israelite's simple, obedient "Hallelujah," which has been used sincerely for over three thousand years, should have degenerated into a stock element in late-twentieth-century caricatures of religion is a fact worth pondering. Maybe there is something in language equivalent to the physicist's concept of entropy. In the laws of thermodynamics, entropy is defined as "a quantity specifying the amount of disorder or randomness in a system bearing energy or information." As energy is expended within a system, none is lost, but the amount available for doing useful work can only decrease. Within such a system, entropy can only increase. The scary part is that the entropy of the whole universe, according to the physicists, relentlessly moves toward maximum. In other words, the universe as a whole shows an irreversible tendency to degenerate toward a state of maximum disorder or randomness. In that state, no useful work can be done.

It sometimes seems as though that is the long-term tendency of language systems, as well: toward a state in which words, for all the energy they retain, have lost the capacity to do useful work. They may conserve energy in the form of material—highly differentiated verbal stuff, or linguistic debris—but they cannot convey meaning or provoke meaningful response. The long-term evolution of "Praise the Lord" seems to fit that pattern.

I'm not ready to draw any conclusions, except that if some factor like entropy is at work in language, as it seems, then it may take the ashes of an old world and the fire of a new before we ever know the whole choir of meaning in the words "Praise the Lord."

# God's Country I

A dvice for a young city slicker setting up his first professional practice in a cozy farm community:

In your pleasant conversations with the townsfolk, while having your lineage traced, while learning that your chimney needs new flashing and your dwelling was originally a "spec home" built by a contractor who subsequently went under, while hearing bracing news about public easements, spider syndrome in Suffolk sheep and grants from the Women's Guild to the Christian School playground fund, you will hear certain phrases recurring. For fleeting seconds these phrases may strike you as creative contributions to the language or at least authentic sentiments. But after several repetitions you'll come to understand that they belong to a kind of public verbal fund from which all the citizens freely draw.

It's called the "Things We Say to Foreigners Fund."

You'll hear, for example, that the town is "a great place to raise kids" and "you don't need to lock your bike." If you question the way taxes are levied or potholes filled, you'll be reassured, "Give it time—you'll settle in." During a paper drive, if you lean against the shed wall to catch your breath you'll be told, "Gonna have to teach you how to work" or ". . . have to put a little hair on your chest" or ". . . make an honest man of you." You won't need an interpreter.

You may need an interpreter when a neighbor tells you: "We like to keep our yards up." That means, we'd like *you* to keep *your* yard up.

And when the wind blows from the direction of the hog farm, some cherry-faced man will smite his chest, suck in the scent and breathe out with a smile: "Ah, fresh air." When you grimace and ask, "What's that odor?" you will hear, *"That* is the smell of *money."* It will become more and more your own smell from that point on.

By the way, don't tell your neighbor you think it's cruel for a side of beef to have to spend its brief, tragic life jammed with a thousand other prodigious excreters in a steaming, stinking quarter-mile-long shed. You'll probably hear the rhetorical question "You like your beef marbled, don't you?" Even if you have an answer, the next phrase you hear may be this: "Don't worry, them cattle got it better than you do." You'll lie awake nights pondering that one. Best leave it alone. You're new.

The phrases I've mentioned so far should be fairly easy to field. You may need help, though, with a pious-sounding question you're likely to hear during your first few weeks in town. If you have conspicuously not fit in, you may hear it asked as long as a year after your arrival. The question: "How do you *like* it here in God's Country?"

It will be clear from the context in which the question is asked—church basement, back stoop, conference room—that the question has nothing directly to do with beer (see "God's Country II"), although you will probably have to dismiss that association before you can think clearheadedly about a response.

Obviously, it would be unwise to reply, "Not very well." It will be equally obvious that, to the speaker, the issue is closed. The issue is not what is or is not "God's Country." This *is* God's Country. The issue is you. How do you *like* it?

Well, that may be a little hard to say. If this new town of yours is "God's Country," then what, presumably, did you leave behind? Sodom? If you're a young dentist or M.D., you may have recent memories of golf outings with other interns or nights at the symphony. If you're a young assistant professor, you may have in mind heroic pictures of yourself battling legions of hostile interrogators at your oral defense. Whatever your place of origin, you're fairly likely to view it as a place where honorable work could be done, where friendships and family could survive, if not prosper, and where God at least made visits from time to time.

"How do you *like* it in God's Country?"

This being Smalltown, U.S.A., the questioner is fairly likely to fall somewhere on the many-banded spectrum of Protestant denominations—Missouri Synod Lutheran, United Church of Christ-Congregational, Southern Baptist, United Methodist, Orthodox Presbyterian, Reformed Church of America, Assembly of God—and to have grown up singing "This Is My Father's World." The song didn't say, "This is my Father's town." So, presumably, the questioner is properly informed about God's whereabouts.

Perhaps, then, he or she is conferring on "God's Country" a more local meaning. If you've been in town for two weeks or more, you may have noticed how much of life revolves around the church—slow-pitch softball, Wednesday-night prayer meetings, ecumenical tent revivals, morning "Coffee Break Ministries," living crèches at Christmas, Young People's Societies, Mary and Martha Society, Cub Scouts, Businessmen's Prayer Breakfasts at 6:30 a.m., prison ministries, weddings, funerals, hymn sings and Vacation Bible Schools, not to mention the services, catechisms, Sunday schools and special programs. If you have not noticed all this church activity, you may be sure that someone has noticed your activity with respect to church. In *this* town, the questioner might be hinting, proudly, there's a whole lot of churchin' goin' on. Are you fer it, or agin it?

Or you may have landed in a "dry county" that has squared off against its wet neighbor at the county line. Could it be that the questioner really said, "How do you like it in God's *County?*"

Naw.

Oh sure, the question could have been asked that way, prejudices dragging like entrails. But it would have been ugly. And you're a professional. I'm sure you clean your ears. You probably heard right: "God's Country."

The simplest interpretation is probably the one that will leave you feeling the most uncomfortable. "How do you like it in God's Country?" probably means, How do you feel about waking up in a town where there is no shoe store or movie theater, where a four-minute walk puts you in a soybean field, where grain elevators pass for skyscrapers, where church bells ring three rounds on Sunday morning—first a wake-up alarm, then a snooze alarm and finally a scolding? How do you feel about teenagers "dragging Main" all Sunday evening, about sidestepping broken glass the next morning, about the town cop hanging out at Casey's General Store? How do you feel about Ladies' Aids and sewing circles and Couples Clubs? Will you come to our pancake breakfasts, our brunches, our pork roasts, our soup suppers? Would you like a pig-in-a-blanket? Do you drink coffee? Do you like pie? Could you eat a "loosemeat tavern"? Can you hit a sacrifice fly? Would you bundle old newspapers? Can you ignore the train whistle? Would you like some sweet corn? Do you have time to chat? How do you feel about depressed property values, the crumbling band shell, the new Wal-Mart? How do you feel about having to provide the cultural and professional life of this community? Can you do that without putting on airs? Can you live in a place where so little is happening, in a state so close to unvarnished nature, in a place so dominated by horizons and crickets and cirrus clouds that we refer to it as "God's Country"? We've done fine without you for 150 years, but we need your numbers, your offspring, your professional expertise—you can't join us, but please DON'T REJECT US!

"How do you *like* it in God's Country?"

I'm not telling you this so you'll painstakingly think about it next time you're asked. Just the opposite. I'm stepping you through it now to save you time and trouble later. Too much thinking and you might develop a stutter.

"How do you *like* it in God's Country?"

The best thing is not to think about it. Just say, "Fine." And if you want to make a good impression, add a reflective "Yup."

# God's Country II

W here I sit, I suppose, is "man's country"—feet up, dust and grass bits plastered to my shins, filling a chair in front of an air conditioner, reeking of lawn-mower gasoline. The Padres are playing some guys in different uniforms.

Then it's commercial time. The volume kicks up, and through heavy eyelids I glimpse a burbling stream, waving grasses and drifting clouds. A voice assures me that the beer in question is

Pure brewed in God's Country.

Now I'm awake. Sure, the beer sounds cold and smooth right now, but what I would really like is God's Country, wherever it is. I can't resist. I'd like to paddle up that frothing river of beer, jump the falls, salmonlike, wade the snaking streams, find the Spring of Beer where God in his bounty makes beer to flow on the evil and the good. A spring in a meadow where chicory and lupine, buttercup and black-eyed susan always bloom, and where the scented breeze ceaselessly murmurs, "Tastes great! Less filling!" A spring in a meadow in a land where it is always weekend, where the big yellow smiley face shines perpetually on the blue-and-green "Right Now."

Bliss—just a swallow away. But, lo, such bliss is with me only to the end of the commercial.

Back in the world of sweat socks and compost heaps, I come to a chain of realizations. First, there's this paradox, kind of fun: no beer could be pure brewed in God's Country, because any land pristine enough to be called "God's Country" would cease to be pristine the moment you slapped a brewery in it.

Of course, paradox is no barrier to an advertiser. In fact, paradox helps sell the product by mystifying it. When the product is placed just beyond reason—in a magic land where beer can be brewed without making the neighborhood smell like a sickroom—a consumer's desire is awakened. The commercial's secret is that the object of desire it proposes is not a simple can of beer. It's a beer in terms of a country, and a beer in a country in terms of God: a God of a country of a beer! The desire it "taps" is thus more than a desire for a drink. It's the desire for a home, for a parent, for a blessing, and, at its metaphysical height, the desire for an eternal, absolute certainty in the guise of a beer.

Anyone watching the commercial can easily imagine sipping a beer in an unspoiled tract of open land. But if you respond to the commercial's appeal, you will have to perform a more radical shift in imagination. Not only must the country and God go *with* the beer for you, you must begin to believe, on some level, that the country of God is *in* the sipping of the beer. A secular Communion must be held, and at its center, the pivotal moment, there must be a miraculous act of transubstantiation. To put it another way, seeing an association between self, country and God must be transformed into sensing an identity between the three.

If you let the ad work you over, you make that shift effortlessly and quite unawares. One second you want to be in God's Country. The next second you're wanting God's Country to be in you. You feel good anticipating it. You *are* God's Country. In some vain way that the advertisers understand, you're God.

To desire the beer and God's Country is to have possessed it already in the imagination and yet to feel the lack of it in the phenomenal world. The pleasure and pain of that desire—if the advertiser wins his bet—will drive you to the refrigerator or the store for a "cold one."

Not for a minute need I assume that "God's Country" refers to any sort of God who could be worshiped. Thirty-five years of intermittent TV watching have taught me what is virtually a Boob Tube Law: No genuine religious sentiment or belief shall enter into any commercial television advertisement. (Cynics would argue that this law applies even to ads placed for religious organizations and causes—they may have more of a point than some of those organizations would like to admit.)

The words *God* and *country,* especially in close conjunction, are so caramel-covered that they completely hide the apple underneath—there need be no apple. They seem to work upon the autonomic nervous system, the brain stem more than the cortex. To hear or say "God's Country" triggers a pleasure reflex. But these sweet words have their opposite counterparts in statements of blind anger or stock prejudice.

"Such statements," says the linguist S. I. Hayakawa, "have less to do with reporting the outside world than they do with our inadvertently reporting the state of our internal world: they are the human equivalent of snarling and purring" *(Language in Thought and Action,* 5th ed., p. 28). Though nothing in the beer ad is true, the ad can't be accused of lying, since its purpose never was to tell the truth, only to purr and hope that purring, like yawning, will be contagious.

I can't help but think, finally, that the process this ad-talk and ad-imagery set in motion will be circular. What starts as seeing beer in terms of God's Country will end with God's Country being seen in terms of beer.

Two guys will be leaning back against their overturned canoe, picking fish bones from their teeth and snapping a pop top. Stirred by a primal memory, one will gaze across the burbling stream at waving grasses and drifting clouds. He'll need words to express the mystical union he feels with nature. "Look at this," he'll say, with a sweep of his arm. "This is God's Country."

"Yeah," the other will say, tutored by TV. "It don't get any better than this."

# Special Music

D eep in the midlands of America—I'm talking about the *spiritual* midlands, which are found on both coasts as well as in the Rust Belt, the Bible Belt, the Grain Belt, the Snow Belt, the Cactus Belt, the Leather Belt and all the other expandable stretches of this spire-spangled land—someone this week is undoubtedly making "Special Music." You won't hear it in a Catholic mass or a censer-swinging high Episcopal service. You won't hear it from the rocking Pentecostals above the rimshots, organ tremolos and lead basses. But if you attend a church anywhere in evangelical or fundamentalist terrain, you might hear "Special Music."

It might be a production number from a Christian musical performed by a robed choir. It might be a violin solo by a gifted thirteen-year-old. It might be a team of bell-ringing women or a men's quintet or a touring duet from a local School of Bible and Music. Heavens, in some churches it might even be an old Amy Grant tape over the P.A. with someone lip-synching the words—tackier things happen.

"Special Music" doesn't have to be any of the above, classic or "Christian contemporary," praise song or traditional hymn, faltering or symphony-smooth. It may be announced as "Special Music" in the "Order of Worship," but it doesn't have to be.

Music becomes "Special Music," according to Dr. Gerald Bouma, professor of music at Westmont College, the moment the congregation is treated as an audience and the music is treated as entertainment. The same piece of music could fall on either side of the fence, depending on how it is used.

One can recognize the "Special Music" moment by a simple test: when it is over, do you feel the obligation to applaud? How different that urge is from the one felt after a musical offertory or an effective sermon. When music is worshipful, it is thought of as emerging from the congregation as an offering to God, and it is integrated with all the other offerings of worship in the service. Acts of worship require no response, because they are already seen as responses, to each other and to God. Music becomes "Special Music," worship's evil twin, when it is offered *to* the congregation, not *by* it, when it is worked into a church service for no intelligible reason other than to satisfy, amuse or impress.

Typically, "Special Music" is plugged in after the offering, when nothing much else is happening. Up to that point the church service may have been designed as worship. But then the paradigm slips. Ta-da. Now it's Ted Mack's "Amateur Hour" or Ed McMahon's "Star Search."

Why doesn't somebody jump up out of the pew next time the "Special Music" is on and yell, "Hey, everybody, can't you see our paradigm's slipping?" Why doesn't somebody object that if performance music is labeled "special" then all the other music in the service—in fact, the rest of the service itself—is rendered *ordinary* by implication? Why doesn't somebody in the pew expose this mediocrity in worship for what it is?

Bouma says that in designing a service he tries to make everything in the service, including the music, contribute to the essential theme of worship, centered in the text for the sermon. The pressure for "Special Music" comes from the pew. "People like it," he says.

Behind that simple, cheerful liking I see quite a number of large forces at work. First, the emphasis on the primacy of the individual heart, mind and soul, that humanistic "holy trinity"—the same emphasis that helped give us the Renaissance, the Protestant Reformation, the many varieties of Romanticism and the U.S. Constitution—has carried over into Protestant middle-class religion, especially evangelicalism and fundamentalism. Evangelicals tend to view the church not as a giant ship so much as a fleet of rowboats and boogie boards, with each individual in search of an authentic personal experience with God.

But worshipers who are seeking absolutely authentic personal experience are more likely to use emotions than ideas as the touchstones of their faith. Their emotions engage the whole organism, not just the head, and don't have the traceable histories that most ideas have. The problem with emotions, especially when they inflate into emotionalism, is that they aren't very sharp at distinguishing causes, effects, reasons and differences. So, in the middle of a worship service, it is not hard to slip unnoticed from adoration of God to adoration of a "Special Musician." Both forms of adoration feel so good.

In order to make a central place for personal emotions in worship, most Protestant groups have cleared away the abstract rubble of high formalism, but they have paid a large price for it: they have lost much of their sense of the *expressiveness* of form. Protestant services, in many cases, are no longer one arcing "song" with numerous motifs. They're potpourris. Public-service announcements replace the call to worship. Interviews with visitors replace responsive litanies. Sermons are prefaced with advertisements for church functions. In the middle of the service, ministers announce that the congregation will now go into "an extended time of worship."

The form of worship inevitably expresses something. If it does not reflect the unity of God or the story of redemption or the unity of the worshipers, it may express the random search for bright ideas or good moments. When the expressive form of worship has been degraded far enough into a series of fits and starts, even those who like their worship plain, direct and loose seem to feel an aesthetic impoverishment. They look around for some form of compensation, and some support a popular kind of ornament that substitutes for aesthetic enrichment: "Special Music."

But why "Special Music"? It's too easy just to say that it follows the TV variety-show format and people like that kind of entertainment, so—hey, why not? Go back further and see how industrialization and professionalization and, lately, digitalization have put the "big picture" out of reach of almost everybody. The world now plunges on, driven by invisible and inaudible engines. Moneyed interests, the information explosion, international intelligence-gathering, inscrutable sciences—all these and more place nearly everyone in the posture of a receiver. Our best human moments occur now in times of war and hurricane and political upheaval, when key individuals can, momentarily, maybe, grasp the reins and act to discover or forge meaning. But on an ordinary day, passivity is the order of human affairs.

Unfortunately for the mentally and spiritually lazy, comments Bouma, worship is work. He's right. It takes effort, seeking, active receiving, synthesizing and commitment. It unsettles the patterns of everyday life and taxes mind, heart and soul even as it builds them up. Even when the liturgies of worship are the same from week to week, worship always bodes change in the person and in the world and acts as a catalyst to bring it about. In other words, worship hurts as it helps.

A mass of people, acting upon mass impulse, will tend to avoid hurt, even the productive kind. A mass of religious people will do the same. But the proven way for masses to avoid the pain of personal encounter with their inmost and outermost lives is to immerse themselves in mass entertainment. Turn on the TV. Crank up the stereo. Go to a movie. The demand for "Special Music," I believe, is one little churchly borrowing of that popular mode of escape. But it's cloaked in the language of faith, so people can avoid their worship and have it too.

That kind of avoidance is directly contrary to the spirit of worship, as I understand it. That, I suspect, is why I feel a little greenish when I am treated to "Special Music," even when the performance is stunning.

# Lifting Holy Hands

I want men everywhere to lift up holy hands in prayer.

1 TIMOTHY 2:8

*I* didn't know the meaning of "heavy-handed" until I moved from a no-hands church to a hands-up church. In the Dutch Calvinist denomination that produced me, everything is done decently and in good order, from the annual synodical fights over women in office to the arrangement of cleaning fluids on a janitor's cart. The order of worship in my home church was printed in the bulletin, and the offertory on the pipe organ was concert-quality Bach. Hands did not fly up, in prayer, in song or in jest. Oh, once a year, in an unfettered moment, the minister might ask for a show of hands, but he would apologize, saying, "We don't normally do this." If a visitor from one of the emotional churches had enthusiastically waved a hand in the air during the singing of, say, "A Mighty Fortress Is Our God," one of the congregation's many M.D.s would probably have clambered to the rescue.

Now I go to an evangelical chapel where hands spend more time up than down, and here my own hands feel like concrete footings.

Up front, the members of the worship team close their eyes and raise Spirit-filled hands at the strum of an electronic chord. My hands fill my pockets. Reluctant hands are prompted upward by the words of the praise songs:

Here we are, in your presence,

Lifting holy hands to you.

Hands wave before me, behind me, all around me. I diddle my keys.

I have secretly vowed to be honest with myself in worship. I will make no gesture before its time. If no mighty rushing wind sucks my hands skyward, I will not raise them just to be in fashion. I have that much late-sixties nonconformism about me. And yet I don't want to be a stiff. If a genuine neoapostolic charismatic impulse overtakes me, I want to be ready. I know that I cannot act spontaneously out of principle—that's a contradiction in terms. But all my unprincipled impulses are dragged before an inner panel of critics before they ever reach my fingertips. The upshot is that my hands never shoot up. All I can do is to stand here singing, swaying slightly, with my fingers doing a Gene Krupa/Buddy Rich thing on the pew in front of me. But I'm ready.

Meanwhile, the last thing I want to do is to peek at others raising their hands. That's voyeurism of the lowest kind. Most unholy. But I confess, in my incorrigibly honest way, that I've cast sidelong glances at the holy hands around me. I've wanted to know how others felt and whether maybe I could feel that way, too. Here is what I've seen:

A's hand unfurls like a small flag.

B pumps his fist in a "right on" salute.

C's hand rotates slowly like a radar dish.

D's hands form a basket overhead, as if to catch a baby.

E holds his hands high, cupped and side by side, as if offering his wrists to be cuffed.

F wags her hand "hello" to God.

G slices the air like one of Hitler's underlings.

H's hand comes up straight and whole, like the red flag on a mailbox.

I's hand springs up quickly and off cue like an ice-fishing flag.

J's swaying body waves her hands like strands of kelp.

K makes a fist behind his head, as bicyclists do at the finish line.

L looks as if he's just heard through a bullhorn: "Come out with your hands up."

M keeps his elbows high as if to have his pockets frisked.

N looks like the guy in the first car on every roller coaster.

O's uplifted face and palms appear to soak in a spring rain.

P, with the outstretched hands, resembles Superman in flight.

Q leans her head along her arm like a swimmer doing the side-stroke.

R might be Rocky on the steps of the Philadelphia Museum of Art.

S's palms cover her brows.

T's hands seem to push away the Evil One.

U's hands support two full bags of groceries.

V's spread fingertips appear to be lifting panels of acoustical tile.

W's arms haul in bales of grace from heaven.

X's fingers twiddle like a belly dancer's with finger cymbals.

Y puts an arm up like the know-it-all at the back of the classroom.

Z conducts a dream orchestra.

If I had more alphabets, perhaps I could go on. I see as many shades of holiness as hands. It would take a Holy Spirit to sort them out, and to the Holy Spirit I defer.

But I am grateful to the minister for reminding us that no one posture is required of the heart. Standing, kneeling, sitting down, raising hands, clapping, tapping fingers on the pews—let it come as the joyful, submissive heart bids. This is what I needed to hear but never heard during all the days of my knit-browed, obedient youth.

I'm standing now as I have always stood in church, with hands in my pockets.

Holy hands.

# Proof Text

hen I hear people speak of "proof texts" from the Bible, I keep one caution in mind: there's a thin line between *proof* and *poof.*

Proof goes poof when people treat the Bible as a magic book. Confused? Anxious? Sick of it all? They flip open the book and accept the first text that strikes their eyes as direct communication from the Lord. "Let the Spirit do the walking." Words in a "poof text" have no history, no context, no community, no layers, no internal stresses, no tendency to evolve, no connotations, no poetry, no echo or shine. These words are not informed by contrasts to other words. Not part of a discourse. Not altered in translation. They are not in any sense efforts or acts. They are hard, priceless, opaque little objects with the mystical ability to make truth present to a reader upon request. In other words, amulets. Talismans. Lucky charms.

What a lovely world that would be, preserved in the joy of child-hood, where we could meander through a yard, chins uplifted, blindfolds on, swinging sticks at a Holy Piñata and waiting for the candy rain.

Proof also goes poof when people use Bible texts as rubber stamps. As far as I can observe, most Christians who refer to biblical proof texts are not consciously committed to magical thinking. Their habit and commitment is to back up what they say with reference to an appropriate verse from Scripture, thus keeping each thought "captive to Christ." As Paul says in his second letter to the Corinthians: "We demolish arguments and every pretension that sets itself up against the knowledge of God, and we take captive every thought to make it obedient to Christ" (10:5). There. I've done it myself.

If a speaker's thought sprang from Scripture, the reference to a text works like a scholarly citation. That's fair. But sometimes a speaker tacks on a proof text as if to say, "See there. That's all the authority I need." The text then works like a touchstone: the speaker dashes a comment against it to show by the color of the streak that the comment is genuine. There may be some unconscious alchemy in this, a carryover of the old magical way of thinking. But citing proof texts this way may also be a carryover of flawed methods from Sunday school, where *collection* and *application* of Scripture are sometimes emphasized over interpretation and understanding. This tendency toward atomizing Scripture and associating one occasion or one thought with one text may be reinforced by religious greeting cards and the popularity of picking "favorite verses."

What's wrong with citing proof texts? First, it's a misuse of "proof." Proof means evidence sufficient to establish the truth or believability of a given proposition. In a strict sense, that means scientifically gathered and validated evidence. In an ordinary sense, proof means evidence enough to be persuasive. By accepting any book as a divinely revealed Scripture, one has already placed oneself and the book out of the range of strictly logical proofs. Furthermore, a single text by itself can't be sufficient proof in either the scientific or the ordinary sense. Evidence used in that way leads to hasty generalizations. Out of context, a single text can actually be dangerous. Think how often Christians have used biblical proof texts to justify racist attitudes, slavery, oppression of women, rape of the earth, exploitation of children, plunder of neighboring lands and warped visions of the end of the world. How many heresies and cults have sprung from the abuse of proof texts.

Major documents of orthodox Christian belief—the Heidelberg Catechism of 1563, for example—supply texts but use them in a different way. They gather clusters of texts from many parts of the Bible and use them to corroborate each other. They don't so much purport to prove a doctrine as to attest its scriptural soundness. In other words, they test Scripture against Scripture. Proof texts, by contrast, sometimes do little more than front for a speaker's preconceptions.

Second, citing proof texts is a misuse of texts. Some people appear to start with faith in the infallibility of Scripture and step from there to what I would call a monadic view of the text. That is, they go from a belief in the truth of the whole to a belief that the whole truth is fully present in every part. If the whole truth is present in every part, then any part of a text, even a single "proof text," can serve as an authority.

Such faith is misplaced. A "proof text" no more constitutes truth than a single biblical proverb constitutes wisdom. Here, for example, is one proverb: "Gray hair is a crown of splendor; it is attained by a righteous life" (Prov 16:31). As I glance at the greasy gray locks of the broken-down homeless man at the bus stop near my house, what is "proved" by a text such as this? Is it a statement of fact? In what sense is it true? Where should one turn to gather the full and best sense of these words?

Words come to a writer loaded with innumerable potential senses that have been established by use. The pertinence of the word—its local meaning—is established by its function in phrases and clauses. But the making of meaning is a reciprocal process: words constitute the meanings of sentences even as sentences color the meanings of words. Moreover, sentences do not possess their own full sense but derive it from the give-and-take between themselves and other sentences, other units of thought, small and large, and other lines of discourse. Discourse, in turn, is driven by passions and restrained by rules, and from the play of oppositions implied in that contest it derives its form. Just as a word contributes some of its potential meaning to a sentence, so the text as a whole contributes a sense to the word. But just as a word derives its exact sense from its context, the text as a whole derives its sense from the community of purpose for which it was composed and from the universe at large.

The word *text* springs from the Latin verb *texere*, "to weave," the same word that gives us *texture* and *textile*. A written text, literally, is a woven thing. Like a tapestry, it is made of many threads, stretched within borders and crisscrossed at points of friction, with gaps in between. The thread in the textile is valued not for itself but for the way it opposes other threads, in order to disappear with them into a higher-dimensional field. We find blue threads in gray fields and gray threads in blue. So with "proof texts." Some may be found whose sense in isolation appears contrary to the sense of the whole; yet, in full perspective, they too may play their part.

If fabric is a fitting analogy for a text, then "proof texting" is a bad idea. It chops up Scriptures into swatches and threads. Scriptures should be read, instead, as they were composed: as a text growing outward in its parts to an emerging vision of the whole, and returning the sweetness of the vision to every part, down to the last detail.

If snippets of Scripture are viewed as small drafts of the vision, then maybe we could speak of them as "proof texts" still, though in a different sense, as we speak of proof in strong drink, 200 being pure.

# Chapter and Verse

*I* will never forget the terse evaluation written by one of my students after a college course called "Visionary Literature": "It was a good course, but I would have appreciated more chapter and verse."

Chapter and verse.

With that phrase the pigeon of guilt landed on my roof. My teaching would have been more authoritative, this student seemed to imply, and probably more fitting for the Christian college where I taught, if I had given biblical proof texts to support my interpretations of the long poems we read. Something in me went "Oops." Successful integration of faith and learning was a criterion for retention and promotion. Was I derelict in my teaching? in my faith? Would I lose my job? Was I really saved?

Guilt was easy to shoo away, but it left droppings of wonder and disappointment, the stains of which have not been easy to remove. Even now, I grow quizzical when I reflect on the young man. He reminded me of the actor Max Von Sydow: whiskery, hazy-voiced, stiffer than a walnut plank, too tall by a head. Whoever had designed the students' desks, the kind with the apostrophe-shaped right arm rests, had apparently not anticipated bones as long as his. He sat crammed in like an umbrella in a napkin ring. Unlike the ruddy Von Sydow, however, he seemed to lack some vital humor. His hands worked like paddles, and he wore a slightly pained expression all the time. Other students' merriment appeared to make him skip a step in some logical proof in his mind, and until the laughter subsided he would smile uncomfortably.

On one hand, his piety came as no surprise. In quick exchanges after class he would home in on my personal concerns and say, "I'll pray for you." Whenever something went right, he was prompt to say, "Praise the Lord." The son of a conservative minister, he himself was heading for seminary. He had the honesty, sincerity and sense of duty that would make him a pastoral success in a little hamlet somewhere. He had what we like to call that Protestant work ethic.

But I was disappointed in him in a way maybe only a teacher who risks something for a student could be disappointed. In our class on "visionary literature" we had studied long prophetic writings such as Dante's *Divine Comedy,* Milton's *Paradise Lost,* William Blake's *Jerusalem,* T. S. Eliot's *Four Quartets* and C. S. Lewis's space fantasy *That Hideous Strength.* One of our guiding questions from the start had been "What might be the contours of a prophetic Christian vision?" In other words, what would major works of Christian visionary insight teach us about seeing the heavenly and the mundane, the vast and the minute, the historical and the contemporary, the evil and the good, the humorous and the grave, the intellectual and the passionate in one all-synthesizing perspective? We were crazy for taking on so much in one semester, but I had the advantage of being young and still foolish behind the ears.

Our class discussions, like the works we read, were dotted with references to the Bible and full of wrestlings with their implications. Genesis. Ezekiel. Daniel. Isaiah. The Gospels. Romans. Apocalypse.

We went for the big picture and for our own pulses all at the same time.

Yet my student wanted more "chapter and verse." The hard stuff.

Okay. Suppose I had granted his wish. Suppose I had dotted my lectures with proof texts. Suppose I had tested every key proposition I had found in Milton, Blake or Eliot against an appropriate touchstone from Scripture. Suppose I had ended every class with a passage suitable for doctrine and reproof. What would I have done? Granted, I could have passed for a Christian college teacher—possibly even a great one. But the joke would have been on me. While teaching a course on "vision," I would have been blind. Worse, I would have communicated my blindness to my students.

What do I mean by scriptural "blindness" and "vision"? Blindness, to me, means reading *in* the Scriptures, collecting passages like marbles. Vision is reading *through* the Scriptures, as through a set of microscopic and telescopic lenses.

Blindness is pointing at the Bible. Vision is seeing where the Bible points.

Blindness is making a false idol of the Bible itself; call it "bibliolatry." Vision is receiving revelation unhampered by -olatries or -isms.

Blindness is accepting boiled-down ideas for the whole truth and nothing but the truth; call it "essentialism." Vision is a reversal of that process: seeing how eternal mysteries in the foundation of things unfold in the marvels of creation.

Blindness is "propositional"; in other words, it mistakes statements of truths (propositions) for truths themselves. Vision is aware of the vast unspoken, even unspeakable, nature of God, the universe, time and words.

Blindness is "magical thinking." It clutches propositions like little amulets, or magic lamps, as if rubbing them could release the genie of meaning. Vision is "mysterious thinking." It probes and embraces full-hearted mysteries. There is nothing magical about it, but it is full to the brim with the supernatural.

Blindness, in other words, is all the ax-grinding, plate-stacking, bean-counting, nose-elevating mediocrity implied in the phrase "chapter and verse." Vision is the opposite.

When I read what I have written here, I think I sound a little defensive, like a guy who never got to answer back. Must be my student touched a sore spot. If his request for more "chapter and verse" signaled a failure of vision, part of the blame must be mine. I had my chance to open his eyes. And I never saw it.

# Amen

S trange, isn't it: the word *amen* is both a closure and an opening. On one hand, it brings a prayer, a benediction or an
inspired speech to a satisfying end. Can you imagine ending
the Lord's Prayer with "For thine is the kingdom and the
power and the glory forever"? You'd ache like a full bladder until
somebody added the terminal "Amen." Yet the meaning of the word,
literally, is something like "Truly," "So be it," "These words are trustworthy and reliable" or simply "Yes." When you say "amen," therefore, you affirm that the words that went before it ought to go right
on speaking. "Amen" shuts the physical mouth but keeps the mouth
of meaning open.

It is possible to get the same effect without the word *amen*. Listen
in. You'll hear a Maine farmer's "Yup." A Southside Philadelphian's
"Absolutely." A Black Panther's "Right on." A surfer's "Bitchin'." A
wise guy's "You got it." A Valley Girl's "Totally." A British barrister's
"Precisely." A tough guy's "Yeah." A Pentecostal's "That's right." A

Spirit-filled evangelical's "Thank you, Jesus." A yuppie's "Exactly." A bureaucrat's "That is correct." And a coffee-drinker's "True."

"Amen," however, is the universal favorite. Charles Panati, in *Extraordinary Origins of Everyday Things,* claims that the Hebrews adapted the word around 2500 B.C. from an Egyptian oath appealing to the highest deity, Amun, "the hidden one." The best dictionaries are not so sure, but they attest that the word is used in many languages around the world. Wherever the Hebrews got it, they made new uses for it as a response to oaths or prophecies or benedictions. David, in the Psalms, even doubles the phrase to "Amen and Amen." The Hebrews lent it to the Christians, who made it part of their informal prayers and formal church liturgy. In the books of the New Testament, by one count, the word makes 119 appearances.

Wherever it appears, in church, at home or on the street, it signifies unity of purpose, unity of understanding, unity of spirit. With our noses in our newspapers, we pay so much attention to political hypocrisy, decaying infrastructures, corrupt banking deals, drug trafficking, gang warfare, racism, greed and all the other things that accelerate the crumbling of society that we fail to see the nearly hidden girders, like our amens, that supply the strength of our best institutions, our purest relationships and our clearest consciences.

Even in these quiet, ordinary functions, *amen* has a strange way of working at both the center and the circumferences of a person's speech. It has to have that fascinating strangeness to remain in such widespread use without hardening into a tiresome cliché. But long ago, as described in the books of the New Testament, the word *amen* was made flesh, and there that strangeness reached apocalyptic proportions. In the prophetic pageant of the apostle John, the resurrected Christ appears to John and instructs him to start a letter to the church in Laodicea this way:

> These are the words of the Amen, the faithful and true witness,
> the ruler of God's creation. (Rev 3:14)

Christ calls himself the Amen: in other words, the Truly, the So Be It, the Trustworthy and Reliable, the Universal Yup. This wordplay is not simply another of the wild obscurities in John's many-layered symbol system. It corresponds with some of the most profound words of the apostle Paul, found in his letters to the Corinthians:

> For no matter how many promises God has made, they are "Yes" in Christ. And so through him the "Amen" is spoken by us to the glory of God. (2 Cor 1:20)

Those prepositions—*through* him the "Amen" is spoken *by* us—have a twisty way about them, but Paul's point, made clearer in the following verse, is that "it is God who makes both us and you stand firm in Christ." In other words, Christ, "the Word," is a believer's concluding verbal response to God's greatness.

*Amen* is, fittingly, the last word in the Bible. It looks ordinary enough there, like the last word in a prayer. But against the background of John's Revelation and the rest of the New Testament, it is stranger than that. One would have to say that *amen* is the Bible's *central* word.

# Lord, I Just Want to Pray

We have a flamboyant artist-friend—some wiseacre once said she looked as if she had a fight with a bolt of cloth and the cloth won—who says she cringes every time she hears Christians use the word *just,* as in the phrase "Lord, I just want to pray . . ." This woman does not scoff at religious things. In fact, she is a leader in the worship life of her congregation, and one of those people who constantly undergird the kingdom of God with their prayers. But she has a militant streak. It showed up in her jewelry designs when, after a tour of churches in war-ravaged El Salvador, she began to combine bullet casings with Christian symbols. And she despises the word *just.*

I wondered at first whether my artist-friend's aversion to *just* was a sort of pet peeve raised to the second power and disguised as aesthetic or social criticism. Some people just have a thing about certain words. My father, for example, detests the word *enjoy.* A waiter set a turkey club sandwich platter in front of him one day and made the mistake of adding the benediction, "Enjoy." It must have struck my father as a subtle conspiracy, hatched in the kitchen, to turn this devout Calvinist into an Epicurean. Later that week when my father related the incident to his family, his indignation nearly blew the tassels off his white golf shoes. He had thoroughly not enjoyed his meal, even with a senior citizen's discount.

But after tuning my ear to our habits of speech for a while, I've concluded that the artist makes a valid point about *just.* In recent months I've heard the same point made by several others.

"Enjoy," for its part, is a benign and stereotypically Italian catch-phrase, like "Ciao" or "an offer he can't refuse," one of many conspicuous phrases that are in with Americans one decade and out the next, depending on what's on TV. Millions of people seem to crave a steady supply of this verbal junk food. I try to limit my intake, but I can't feel much more than pity for those who overindulge.

*Just* can spread through a similar process of mindless replication. However, when *just* attends church, it cuts a different figure. It is not a conspicuous catchphrase. It tries to hide from view. But like a family that invariably occupies the back seat in a balcony, it draws attention to itself by its very effort to be rendered invisible. So it disturbs people like my friend.

I'm not referring to standard usages of the word. In some contexts, like the following, *just* works smoothly and inconspicuously:

☐ Just [no more than] a minute, you guys.
☐ Darn it, I just [precisely this moment] spilled custard on my tie.
☐ I'll just [simply] step out for a moment, if you don't mind.
☐ Add just [exactly] enough cornstarch to allow the gravy to thicken.

But listen to the difference when an evangelical congregation is agonizing over the tumor recently diagnosed in the breast of a young mother. The pastor, rising on the swell of the congregation's collective anguish, prays, "Lord, I just ask that you strike this affliction from her body."

The supplication is undoubtedly sincere. But is "just asking" better than just "asking"? Why this mincing mereness?

Listen when the Sunday-school teachers bow their heads in a round-robin prayer before going off to teach. Every person in the room is a fervent Christian. Their discovery of the power of prayer has become a quiet miracle in many of their lives. The leader prays, in a tone of sincere submission, "Lord, I just praise your majesty." Another, with lifted face, prays, "Lord, I just thank you that you have brought each of us safely through the snow." Others pick up the word.

Pretty soon, *just* makes its mealy little mark wherever sincere Christians make bold to speak in the presence of the Almighty.

☐ We're just really grateful to have Brother Echevaria with us this morning.

☐ Will you just turn to number 346 and just sing out.

Admittedly, in these contexts, *just* conveys certain feelings of warmth and softness and submission. With a certain exquisiteness, it reflects the combined state of emotional urgency and spiritual vulnerability characteristic of new Christians who stand in half-dazed thankfulness that salvation has come to them by grace alone. God has ravaged their lives for the good. They live with emotionally upstretched hands, aware that their praise is only a leaf to the sunshine of God's infinite worth. Such feelings of submission may flower into a sense of Christian community.

However, the word *just* does not invariably spring from such pure feelings. It may serve a more protective design. Christian in-groups use many forms of inclusive speech to mark their borders. It holds the Christians in and keeps the non-Christians out. A speaker may suppose that a mood of urgent humility is obligatory wherever Christians are gathered together. The word *just* does the trick. In many circles, furthermore, mood tends to outrank message in a speaker's priorities. *Just,* since it conveys no rational meaning, helps simply to sustain the mood of urgent humility. Thus one *just* is allowed to breed another. By the time "justs" begin to breed "just reallys" and "just sort ofs," then the process has begun to smother all rational sense under downy blankets of emotional redundancy. Such an invocation of humility in excess of the practice of it is not a true but rather a sentimental form of piety.

I can't speak for God, but I can't imagine that he is any more pleased with such speech than I am pleased with the fungus that thrives in the warmth of my shower. I was forcefully reminded one day while scanning my radio dial that it is not necessarily at all the language of honest praise or contrition. A serial murderer named Hardy, being interviewed about the motive for his crime, told the reporter: "I would kind of just pray to God and the devil to see who was more powerful." *Just,* evidently, is an equal-opportunity fungus.

Genuine Christians do display the hallmark of humility, but they are guided by the Holy Spirit to be humbly bold and boldly humble. "Humble yourselves before the Lord," writes James (4:10), "and he will lift you up." The writer of Hebrews says, "Let us then approach the throne of grace with confidence, so that we may receive mercy and find grace to help us in our time of need" (4:16). "For you did not receive a spirit that makes you a slave again to fear," says Paul in his letter to the Romans (8:15), "but you received the Spirit of sonship."

When a Christian is well balanced between the humility due to God's greatness and the self-confidence derived from being God's adopted son or daughter, one should expect that person's speech to give evidence of that balance. Such speech will not be whiny or mealy or mincing. It will need no sentimental cushioning. I suppose it will be direct and plain. It will mean just what it says.

☐ Lord, I praise your majesty.

☐ Lord, I thank you that you have brought each of us safely through the snow.

☐ Will you turn to number 346 and sing out.

Can you imagine Martin Luther, always humble before God and bold before humankind, standing before the Diet of Worms in 1521 and proclaiming: "Here I stand. I just cannot do otherwise"? George Bush, maybe. But Martin Luther? No way.

# ADDRESSING THE DIVINITY

# Lord,

M r. Pryor, would you mind telling the court where you were on the night of April 23rd?

April 23rd? I was at home.

And what were you doing at home, Mr. Pryor?

Nothing special. It was an ordinary night.

An ordinary night.

Yes. As far as I can recall, yes. A hot dogs and macaroni kind of night.

Hot dogs and macaroni? Mr. Pryor, could you explain to this court why—

Objection, Your Honor. I fail to see the relevance of this line of questioning.

Your Honor, the scene I am trying to establish will be essential to the jury's understanding of my client's charge of abuse of privilege. May I continue?

Objection overruled. Counsel, be brief.

Very well. Isn't it true, Mr. Pryor, that you prepared hot dogs and macaroni that night to expedite supper because you were expecting a visitor?

Well, yes.

In fact, Mr. Pryor, did you not have a rather large number of visitors that night?

OK, yes, that's true. The 23rd would have been a Wednesday, as I recall.

That is correct, Mr. Pryor. It was a Wednesday. And will you tell the court what is special about Wednesday nights at the Pryor household?

Well, on Wednesday nights each week a Spiritual Growth Group meets at our house.

At your invitation?

Yes.

And the purpose of a "Spiritual Growth Group" is—

You know, to get to know each other, share joys and concerns, study the Scriptures, stuff like that.

Aren't you forgetting something, Mr. Pryor?

Like what?

Prayer. In fact, Mr. Pryor—may I call you Neil?—don't you and the other members of your Spiritual Growth Group customarily pray long and intensely at these meetings? Don't you, in fact, bow your heads and close your eyes and ask fervently for such things as forgiveness of your sins, healing of your diseases and traveling mercies?

Well, sure. That goes on. Lots of people do. I don't see what's wrong with—

The defendant will confine his answers to direct responses to Prosecution's questions.

Thank you, Your Honor.

Counsel, proceed.

Well, then, Neil, how would you describe your role in this group, Neil? Huh, Neil?

It's my house.

Oh, come on, Neil. Don't you perform a somewhat more influential role, Neil, than simply that of homeowner and doorman? Aren't you in fact, Neil, a leader of this group, Neil, and something of a spiritual model? Don't you actually *lead* in prayer, Neil, and by your example, Neil—

Objection, Your Honor! By reiterating the witness's name beyond any reasonable standard of polite address, Prosecution is badgering the witness!

Counsel?

Your Honor, the mode of my address to the defendant is not malicious but rather rhetorically demonstrative and is necessary to my appeal to the jury to empathize with the feelings of my client in direct response to the behavior of the defendant on the night in question.

Your explanation sounds ingenious, Counsel, but I fail to see the point of this "demonstration." Objection sustained. Pursue another line of questioning.

Very well then. Mr. Pryor . . . Neil . . . are you a personal friend of the television entertainer Ed McMahon?

Objection, Your Honor! This is frivolous.

That remains to be seen. Overruled.

Your Honor, I protest that I am being badgered by the objections of the Defense.

Just get to the point, Counsel. The witness will answer the question.

Me? A personal friend? No. I don't know Ed McMahon.

Have you ever received a letter from him?

Never.

Never?

Of course not. Well, unless you count that junk mail from the Publishers Clearing House.

Exactly, Mr. Pryor. You were offered ten million dollars, were you not, if you were the lucky winner of the Publishers Clearing House Annual Sweepstakes?

Ach, I don't pay any attention to that stuff.

Exactly, Mr. Pryor. And do you remember the exact words with which Mr. McMahon addressed you in that letter?

Oh, something about "Congratulations, Neil N. Pryor"—my name was typed in big computer-dot letters—"you may never have to work another day in your life!" Something like that.

Were you surprised that Mr. McMahon knew your name, including even your middle initial, which I suspect not even your best friends know?

Naw, come on. It was from a computer. It didn't mean a thing.

And did he use your proper name only once?

No. He used it over and over again. Every time there was a break in the action. Listen, I'm not fooled by advertising stunts like that. "Neil N. Pryor . . . Neil N. Pryor . . ." Geez, pretty soon my eyes start to glaze over.

Quite understandable, Mr. Pryor. But isn't it true that on the night of the 23rd of April, when your Spiritual Growth Group met in your rumpus room, you led the group in a prayer to the Lord? Isn't it also true that in your prayer, as we have heard from the private testimony of several witnesses, you addressed the Lord as follows—Your Honor, I read here from a sworn statement which I ask to be placed in the record—"Lord, I just come to you right now, Lord, and lay all of these burdens on you, O Lord. Father, in your infinite mercy, O Lord . . ."? Isn't it true, in other words, that you used the word *Lord* in your prayer as practically nothing more than a comma? Used it not, in fact, to address the Lord God Almighty but to mark pauses and fill dead air? Wouldn't you agree with me, Mr. Pryor, that the knowledge of a person's name is something of a sacred privilege which should not be abused? Wouldn't you agree that when you badger me by using my name unthinkingly, you do a certain kind of violence to my person? But isn't it true, Mr. Pryor—Neil—that just as I abused your name a little while ago, and just as Ed McMahon abused yours, so on the night of April 23rd you abused the Lord's name? Do you attempt to deny, before this court, that on that night, by your unthinking use of a name, you caused the Lord's eyes to glaze over?

(Pause)

Answer the question, Mr. Pryor.

I . . . I don't know what to say, Your Honor. I didn't mean to . . .

No one ever means to, Mr. Pryor. Your Honor, if I may, I would like to ask the defendant whether he can identify the Lord in this courtroom. Mr. Pryor, would you look around the courtroom, and if you can identify anyone here, beyond doubt, as the Lord God Almighty, would you point to him? . . .

Let the record show, Your Honor, that the defendant has identified my client. I have no further questions.

# A Heart for Missions

A head for figures.
    An ear for languages.
    An eye for bargains.
    Cheekbones for modeling.
A nose for news.
A chin for boxing.
A back for lifting.
The stomach for police work.
A heart for missions.

# Reaching the Unchurched

D ear Rev. Smughart:

You don't know me, but I live just downwind of your little operation. I try not to pay much attention to what goes on there. I don't mind your organ tones and kids screaming and all those happy people making small talk, as long as you don't mind my stereo and the occasional sound of happy people making small talk on my patio over barbecue and beer.

What I do mind is Sunday-school papers blowing into my hedge. Generally, I pick them out on Monday morning and throw them away. I've got three kids of my own and I'm not about to have them propagandized by the wind. Not to mention that I keep a neat garden and don't need your construction-paper angels for mulch.

I don't usually say a word about your little "gifts." I just let my husband have it in the ear, and he says, "Keep it low-key. Don't give them an excuse for coming over here." So that's what I do. But yesterday I picked up a blue sheet that was harpooned on my dwarf thornapple. All day it left me doing a slow burn, so I decided to let you have it in the ear for once and spare my husband.

It must be your Sunday-school superintendent who wrote this—I have it in front of me. It's a letter to your teachers that says, among other things, "Let's make next month the month when we all make a special effort to reach the unchurched." It says you're going to be knocking on doors all around the neighborhood inviting "unchurched" children to your Sunday-morning classes.

Now do me a favor, will you? Please, don't refer to me or my husband or any of our three children as "unchurched." You may refer to us as non-Christians. That is true. Not one of us is a believer in your God. None of us intend to be. None of us are followers of your Jesus. We are not impressed by followers of Jesus and, frankly, have other plans. Or you may say—because it is the truth—that we are not churchgoers. Any of that sort of language I could accept, but the word *unchurched* leaves me with a certain icky feeling and a special kind of wariness of all your happy programs.

Now you may say, "She's a bitter woman. No one will be able to reach her until her sin-hardened heart is cleansed"—you see, I think I know a little how you speak. But you will be mistaken. I am not bitter. And though I say I do not want you coming to my door "reaching out" to my "unchurched" children, I do not mean that you should not come over. Come. But come as neighbors. Neighbors don't reach out. They visit. Come to share a beer with me and see how I clip my roses. That's how my friends come. Send your children here to play, and invite my children there for the same purpose. Children like to play, and there's no harm in it.

Are you unable to do that? Why? Are you afraid to lose your edge? I, for one, would like you better without it. My husband agrees. And if you lost yours, you might find that we were losing ours.

There's more. You might assume that because we're not impressed by followers of Jesus, we're not impressed with Jesus. That's not so. We've heard and read about a lot of religions in our lives. We've taken good from many of them. We're good people and we live clean lives.

But through it all we have felt dissatisfactions stirring and longings for something deep to happen that would change us both. We don't know what it is, but we've talked about it together and both of us, my husband and I, have said that Jesus has the least claptrap about him and the strangest way of stirring our sense of wonder. That's not faith, mind you, but at least it's respect. Nobody talks quite the way he does about being the Way, the Truth and the Life. I've heard it said that he'd either have to be what he said or he'd have to be a damn fool. And I'm not ready at all to say he's a fool.

So, OK, some little part of us has paid attention to your God. But we would want him raw. We wouldn't want him processed. We don't want to have to wade through bulletin boards and Christmas programs and collection plates and businessmen's prayer breakfasts and flannelgraphs and pulpit furniture and bouquets and award dinners and hymn sings and blah blah blah blah blah. You see, if you refer to us as the "unchurched," you're making us the opposites of you. Then I guess you must think of yourselves as the "churched." In other words, processed. Confined. Stuck in a place. Defined by a place, even a church building. If you've got an official piece of paper in a file cabinet somewhere, you're all right for eternity. If you haven't got the paper, you're all wrong.

Do you honestly believe that once we've tasted the pleasure of noninstitutionalized friendships, the freedom of conscience we now enjoy and the satisfaction of raising our children in their own natural way, we would ever want to trade it all in for your tight little two-step? Far better for your sake that you would first find out what we know. Then you would be able to make a choice that right now you seem incapable of making. You'd be able to choose whether to be churchpeople or Christians.

I'll make a deal with you. If you can first become un-churched, I'll become un-unchurched. Sound fair? Ha! The only reason I dare make a deal like that is because I know you can't do it.

Like I said: I'm not against your coming over. But don't come over unless we've got a deal.

I'm enclosing the blue paper that started all this. It got a little wet but I used a hair dryer on it and an iron. I've circled the phrase that got me going. Sorry about all the crayon marks. That's my Renata. She's three.

Your neighbor, with no hard feelings,
Bernice Cinder

# Prayer List

W hich of your friends and family have ever told you that you were at or near the top of their prayer list?
1. Clark
2. John
3. My mother
4. Pete and Marion (who count as one)

What are your first reactions upon being informed that you have made a prayer list?

1. Embarrassment
   a. that my private life is another person's concern
   b. that I have become such a problem as to require intercession
   c. that I have not kept a list of my own
2. Fear
   a. that the way I feel to myself may not be the way I appear to others
   b. that someone may know my needs better than I know my own

c. that prayer will be efficacious and my life will change
3. Resentment
   a. that someone is meddling with my spiritual welfare
   b. that someone else has grabbed the inside track to God
4. Gratitude
   a. that my private life is another person's concern
   b. that someone knows my needs better than I know my own
   c. that someone has found the inside track to God
   d. that prayer may be efficacious and my life will change

Why did the towheaded Clark, a musically and verbally gifted but socially ill-at-ease high schooler, maintain a prayer list?

1. He was such an avid listener and so extraordinarily attuned to the inner strivings of his many acquaintances that he needed a list to manage all the spiritual data he collected.

2. He was uncomfortable among athletes and high-school socialites; he wanted a different body and a different life. Out of sync with himself, he often resorted to mechanical cures, such as point systems to monitor his use of clichés or Benjamin Franklinish programs of moral improvement. He became a classic codependent, subservient with a desire to master, affectionate with an undercurrent of jealousy. A prayer list served him well, for it placed other lives before his yet required his own effort to make them work.

3. He was the son of a missionary, hymn writer and administrator of a Bible college. Prayer lists were bequeathed to him among other articles of the family business.

4. He was kind, selfless, generous, good and sincere enough in his belief in God that he could be disciplined in making intercession for his fellow believers.

Why did a short, black, precocious Pentecostal organist like John keep you at the top of his prayer list?

1. The novelty of meeting a white kid like me at Interlochen National Music Camp and building a lasting friendship around music, race and Christianity never wore off. Our brotherhood re-

mained such an improbable spectacle that my name would not yield to a lower spot on his list.

2. My baptism as an infant and public profession of faith as a teenager did not qualify me as "saved" in Pentecostal terms. I needed to show the evidence of being "born again." I needed baptism in the Spirit, the gift of tongues, testifying in church, healing, prophecy, etc. "Randy," he would say, "when you get saved, there's gonna be SHOUT marks on the wall!" Nevertheless, my orthodox Calvinist rearing and conviction of my own salvation had apparently brought me near enough to "saved" in his terms that I belonged at the top of his list, where he could get the most conversion bang for his prayer buck.

3. He did not, in fact, keep me at the top of his prayer list but told me he did so that my conscience would dog me into the arms of the Lord.

Does your mother really place you near the top of her prayer list?

1. Yes. But her prayer lists are like grocery lists: sketchy, lost and finally inconsequential because the groceries she brings home are double the number of items on the list. Somewhere on there, I guess, between the milk and the pickled peaches, is me.

2. No. Being a right-brained and slightly dyslexic artist, she is not given to methodical procedure in anything except the creation of a watercolor. Her "lists" are more like pools of concern, irregular in outline and spring-fed. When she has said at the difficult intervals in my life, "Your dad and I are praying for you," I did not picture her consulting a list. I pictured the two of them kneeling by their bed, praying in harmony, and I pictured them going about their day, aching.

How do you respond when Pete and Marion say they have you on their prayer list?

1. Embarrassed, slightly fearful and grateful, but never resentful.

2. Charmed, as I am charmed by the systematic work of industrial engineers. Pete and Marion not only write down, on paper, the names of those they are praying for, but they will follow through

and write down, on paper, how those prayers have been answered.

3. Awestruck, because their engineering is entirely focused on knowing and doing the will of the Lord. Their offers of prayer are pure gifts—with the price tags removed. I had never suspected how the keeping of lists could be made compatible with joy in the Spirit, but if I am ever to learn, I suspect it will be from Pete and Marion.

# Spiritual Warfare

*I* want to talk about "spiritual warfare," the phrase and the thing, yet the words will not come. After months of listening, reading and reflecting on the subject, I seem to have nothing to say, though I don't really trust the way things seem.

Now I have turned off my desk lamp and darkened my computer screen until these letters that trail my flashing cursor are barely visible. In this way, I'm chopping myself off from the pressure world of desktops, deadlines and duties. If I am barren, I want to feel my barrenness. For it is here, to one's personal wilderness, for forty days and nights if need be, that one must go to meet the tempter.

In this gloom I feel more the presence of spiritual powers than I did a paragraph ago. I have sunk halfway out of time, and in this desert twilight I feel the contours of my self more vividly, flaring against the falling cold, sparkling around the edges. I am in friction with this place, and in myself I feel friction. Now I hear the sounds: whisperings, gibberings, proud speeches, clanging of metal on metal, rattling of coaches and roars of jet planes. Hisses and shrieks. Laughter of triumph and laughter of derision. Whipcracks. Kisses. Music, discordant and sweet.

As I withdraw from my world, these noises pursue me from over the horizon.

What's going on over there?

What's going on in here?

Is there a war on?

\* \* \*

On a Christian college campus, a humorless, blond, clean-shaven young man gets up at an open forum to speak about "Spiritual Warfare." As another student might speak of parental divorce, abusive behavior or alcoholism, he speaks of his father's long descent into Satan worship. He has been there. He has suffered. And by his prayers and counsel he has had to help rescue his father from demon possession. He is not able to describe all that he has seen, but he reports to the hushed students in the hall that Satan and his demons are absolutely real and fighting with the legions of God for possession of our souls.

At the same meeting, a well-respected religious studies professor tells how in an urban church he once met a contract killer who said he wanted to become a Christian. But when the man began praying to receive Christ, according to the professor, the man's voice changed into a weird "computer voice" and his face became all distorted. The professor recalls how he prayed: "I charge this religious-sounding spirit to leave you." Shaken, I do not note the outcome; I am too busy trying to visualize that distorted face.

Other students in the audience report bouts of spiritual conflict in which they knew with all certainty that no ordinary melancholy or depression was gripping them. Rather, a demon with all the wiles of C. S. Lewis's Uncle Screwtape was personally dragging them down.

As these dark testimonials are given, there is a hush in the room and some palpable fear, a triumphant sense of power in hand, power to command demons by voicing the name *Jesus,* along with some waves of skepticism that one can sense as hardly anything more than a shifting in a chair.

These are modern-day evangelical young people, thrilled and a bit nervous at claiming for themselves the old apostolic power. As Jesus said at the Great Commission: "And these signs will accompany those who believe: In my name they will drive out demons" (Mk 16:17).

Though I count myself a believer, I have never seen a devil. I have the suffocating knowledge of Hitler's genocide, Stalin's prison camps, Pol Pot's killing fields, Saddam Hussein's murderous regime, the cold-blooded gunfire on Los Angeles streets and my own unloveliness. But I have never seen a devil walking about as a roaring lion or black latex gremlin, never heard one speak in a computer voice, never seen the chandelier shake or the bed rise. I'm not ducking these experiences, but neither have I been encountering them in my life.

Yet I cannot considerately doubt that these students and their professor have seen personifications of evil close at hand and know, more than I do, of its power. They plant themselves in the heart of Paul's famous words to the Ephesians: "Put on the full armor of God so that you can take your stand against the devil's schemes. For our struggle is not against flesh and blood, but against the rulers, against the authorities, against the powers of this dark world and against the spiritual forces of evil in the heavenly realms" (Eph 6:11-12).

Like many in the audience, I am impressed and disturbed. At this intensified moment, it has become easier to imagine that every cynical, distorted thought in our minds has been whispered into being by a wildly grinning, barbecued, pitchfork-wielding demon. And that every faithful or forgiving thought has wafted upon us from the fragrant stroke of an angel's wing. Madness is more an option now than it had seemed an hour ago. A suicidal precipice, with crablike motion, has scuttled backward, close to our very toes, as we grasp for a saving trapeze.

However, something in the presentations seems awry. I think it's the language. The most earnest here have adopted a special vocabulary of spiritual warfare, borrowing much from the Bible. They say words like *armor, battle, claiming, binding, anoint, rebuke, cast out* and *rejoice*. Power words. Verbal hot buttons. Words they would scarcely use in any other setting. They seem hard-pressed to think of spiritual warfare except in terms such as these. One student warns us all of the danger of demonic influence in a game like "Dungeons and Dragons." It strikes me that he, with his dramatic, quasi-apostolic jargon, may be playing in a participatory drama of his own, an angelic parallel. What should I call it? How about "Mansions and Messiahs"?

He speaks, after the apostle Paul, of the necessity for Christians to "take captive every thought to make it obedient to Christ" (2 Cor 10:5). But sometimes even those who are the most earnest seem to become captive in a less desirable sense: captivated by, or stuck on, a specific, approved terminology, and laboring under the spell of those words. I am left meditating on the difference between the Bible's "slavery" to Christ, which is, paradoxically, freedom, and a certain enthrallment with language which is still a form of servitude and, I believe, a muting of the Spirit.

\* \* \*

The recent urgency in debate about spiritual warfare on Christian college campuses such as my own draws upon the phenomenal success of the fantasy novel *This Present Darkness* (1986) by Frank E. Peretti, along with its popular sequel, *Piercing the Darkness* (1989). *This Present Darkness,* somewhat after the fashion of C. S. Lewis's well-known space trilogy, unfolds a spiritual drama of cosmic scope starting from quite ordinary circumstances. In the nondescript little American town of Ashton, a newspaper editor begins to inquire into certain odd happenings in his life and the lives of people around him: bad dreams, disappearances, strange faces, an estranged daughter . . . At the same time, the prayerful young pastor of a small fundamentalist church encounters vandalism, more bad dreams and what looks like a theologically liberal conspiracy against him, aided and abetted by members of his own church council.

These disturbances, it turns out, are but feathers on the shaft of a New Age conspiracy to control minds and souls, not only of the editor's daughter and the pastor's church but also of the police force, the local college, the town and ultimately the world. As a small "remnant" of believers prays for its life, the New Agers network and lie and seduce and extort and conspire and meditate. As the editor recalls, "each of them had this weird gooney-eyed thing they did" (p. 83).

Meanwhile, for every action on earth there is corresponding drama on the spiritual plane. An army of bumbling, brawling devils sends its shock troops to disturb both the good guys and the bad, as a few guardian angels nervously watch and make sure the remnant suffer no burdens greater than they can bear. The faithful defend against the forces of evil and call angels to their aid by building a "prayer cover," which is the more effective as it grows thicker, reinforced by greater numbers. The most effective at prayer is an elderly woman who has had experience in many spiritual wars, including some on the mission fields abroad. Her prayers reflect the pure fundamentalist jargon of spiritual warfare: "Lord God, I build now a hedge around this young couple, and I bind the spirits in Jesus' name. Satan, whatever your plans for this town, I rebuke you in Jesus' name, and I bind you, and I cast you out!" This woman, with her FC (Fundamentalistically Correct) language, establishes the spiritual baseline for righteousness in the story.

The disproportionate spiritual strength of the small band of the faithful provokes the captains and finally the generals of the demonic forces to attack in full fury. A titanic struggle results between the forces of the angels, behind the majestic Tal, and the demonic legions, under the sulfurous, leathery, majestically hideous Rafar. The whole spiritual war, in a nifty bit of plotting, is simultaneous with a human battle-royal over a corrupt attempt to sign over Ashton's local college to a New Age corporation.

Dismiss it as bad literature or bad theology, if you will, but many

Christian college students love this book. As one college chaplain has remarked, some college students would find it easier to criticize the Bible than their Peretti. Not long ago, they would arrive for the fall semester with *This Present Darkness* tucked in their backpacks. They think it's "awesome." And as members of the TV, cinema and video generation, they believe it because they can see it. They don't have to think a lot because the good guys (fundamentalist ministers, blue-collar prayer teams, little old ladies) and the bad guys (intellectuals, liberals, meditators, corporations) are clearly labeled. Everything that could be identified as "New Age"—and that includes Eastern mysticism, reincarnation, karma, mantras, divination, the occult, demon possession, witchcraft, hypnosis, cosmic consciousness, meditation, Science of Mind, psychics, séances, channeling, out-of-body experiences, altered states of consciousness, ESP, telepathy, auras, spirit guides, ascended masters, fortune telling, carnivals, holistic education, self-actualization, yoga, the lotus position, relaxation, concentration, even breathing—is conveniently lumped into one universal Master Plan that looms like a thunderhead over the blond heads of Middle America.

Omni Corporation, an antiseptic front for this worldwide conspiracy of evil agents, is a creature of paranoid fancy. Though it is frightening in the aggregate, it is reassuring, in a certain odd way, because its plug can be pulled by a few devout people at prayer. Moreover, the conspiracy is easily resisted by any reader of sound mind because it gets the ooga-booga treatment to an almost laughable degree. In fact, the treatment somewhat resembles that of the pinwheel-eyed deviates in the 1940s antimarijuana film *Reefer Madness,* which was hooted right into cult fame. I'm tempted to suggest that Peretti retitle his book *Rafar Madness.*

Peretti's demons, though cartoonish, pose a threat, but it's a threat of human dimensions, constituted by scenes of lurking, raging, threatening and invisible flybys. Bracing themselves against that imagined kind of physical assault, readers may have a hard time spotting, much less questioning, the book's deeper assumptions, which seem to me to be separatist, anti-intellectualistic, dualistic and triumphalistic. Here, in a collection of melodramatic equations, big equals powerful. Ugly equals evil. The color black equals bad. Stormy equals spiritually ominous. In depictions such as these, the material world comes in for a beating and is largely aligned with the devils, while its opposite, the spiritual world, is aligned with winged sentiments.

According to C. S. Lewis, in his preface to *The Screwtape Letters,* "there are two equal and opposite errors into which our race can fall about the devils. One is to disbelieve in their existence. The other is to believe, and to feel an excessive and unhealthy interest in them. They themselves are equally pleased with both errors."

Some college students, falling prey to the latter error, already tend to mistake the conventional nightmares of young adulthood for demonic oppression. Peretti's book isn't likely to help. The author asks us to believe both too much and too little.

Shallow art or distorted theology, as the case may be, Peretti's novel nevertheless makes interesting sociology of religion. It offers a McCarthy-like blacklist of spiritual allegiances which includes almost everything that is not Bible-believing, born-again, prayer-chain fundamentalism. Thus part of the Christian community paints itself into a spiritual corner to provoke itself to rear up and fight.

Admittedly, in contemporary society Christians catch some heavy doses of scorn, even though—or possibly because—they are in the vast majority. However, they do not require conspirators and international intrigues for the embarrassment of their public figures; in recent years, many prominent evangelists have taken care of that quite nicely themselves. The truth may be that because of their timidity and venality and rampant cuteness, Christians are commonly and deservedly dismissed in modern society. To compensate, I suppose, they tell stories such as Peretti's in which they are taken seriously. It is easier to be hated than ignored.

Christian young people have an understandable longing to be engaged in an enterprise of great moment, something earth-shaking, something crucial. Muscular Christian spiritual warfare promises all that and more, and is far more attractive to the neophyte than the arduous, humbling and all-demanding process of discipleship that mature Christian institutions promote. In admiring our reflection in cartoon scenarios of spiritual warfare, with holy haves on one side and heinous have-nots on the other, we may be revealing a wish to have our persecution and bear it too.

A wider grasp of Christian revelation commits a person to the proposition that there are no haves, except One. He himself wept, starved and suffered humiliation, without drawing a sword. He prayed, not so that his angels would build an SDI-style "prayer cover" over his head but, as he said, so that he could know and do his Father's will. Those prayers pretty well blew his cover. The forces of evil he toiled against were only in part the ravages of shrieking devils upon disordered minds. Less spectacular, but just as close to the heart of the Christian faith, was his fight against a variety of more ordered evils: indifference and pride of purse, impatience, legalism and snobbery, chronic disease and shortsightedness, nationalism and spiritual deafness, rigidity, hypocrisy, religiosity, violence, treachery, unjust regimes and preoccupation with things. He fought, in short, against the whole empire of death that such devils as there may be have chosen for their eternal home. And his weapon was not fire, sword or moral majorities, but love supreme.

\* \* \*

During the last several years, as the formerly pumped-up U.S. economy staggered out of a decade of greed through a plaza littered with cracked and fallen superheroes—Boesky, Milken, Bakker, Swaggart, Keating, Trump—there was a moment when I seriously wondered whether exorcising would become to the nineties what exercising was to the eighties. Ordinary material success was losing its entertainment value. The entertainment we needed, in our approach to the millennium, would thus have to be spiritual and extraordinary.

And there it was, popping up in novels, in churches, on cable TV.

Under the name *spiritual warfare.*

Older than the history of the world, it came emblazoned with a neon yellow sticker: "NEW!"

I was not buying the new model. I already had an older one. And I wondered whether I would have to watch the commercial parade march on without me.

I am content to do that.

But recently, in a quiet moment—one of those very quiet moments where you discover a lost ring while searching for a sock—I came to the realization that even if I, personally, tend to shrink from dramatic accounts of full-armored battle, I am not excused from spiritual war. It rages within and without, sometimes with bombast, more often with slow poisons, powerful antidotes and gentle salves.

In the darkness of my study now, with my face underlit by the phosphorescence of my computer screen, I can sense that not only am I in the battle. The battle is in me. It rides on every word and on all these words on words.

# Goodby and Good Luck

Goodby and good luck. Goodby and good *luck?!*

Come on. Fish or cut bait.

A short history: *Goodby* is a shortened form of "God be with ye." It may once have been a blessing by a priest upon departure, but from the time it first caught on in public, it seemed bound to be compressed into one word. That word taxed the inventiveness of Elizabethan spellers: god be wy you, god b'uy, god by you, god-buoy, god b'wy. A real mouth full of marbles. Along about the late 1600s, *God,* following the usual route, got generalized into *good,* partly because people usually said "Good day," "Good night" and "Good morrow," and partly, I suppose, because good is more soothing to handle on a daily basis than God. By 1800, as more and more people read more periodicals and books, spelling became less creative, and editors, after toying with good-buy, good-b'wy, good b'w'ye and good-bwi't'ye, finally settled on goodby.

The only major innovation since then has been the adult acceptance of the baby word *by-by,* which, obviously, has neither *God* nor *good* left in it. In our leavetakings today, we sometimes go for color. Ciao, baby. Catch ya later. Adios. Aloha. Take care. Break a leg. See ya later, alligator. Kiss kiss. I'm outta here. But when we mean business, it's still goodby. And behind it you can faintly hear that ancient benediction "God be with ye."

Goodby and good luck?

"Luck," as we know, is a Lady, a blind one. She's a shot in the dark, a pig in a poke, a crapshoot. She goes in streaks, she runs and turns, she breaks. She goes from bad to rotten. With mascots, rabbits' feet and magic hats, men of fortune spin her wheel. Perhaps, perchance, whatever happens, they cast lots, willy-nilly, draw straws, pitch pennies, cut for aces, all for her. As Luck would have it, she's a fluke, a lucky shot, heads or tails, a fat chance. She's in the lotto, at the track, in the pot. Combined with pluck she beats the odds. Come on, buddy, pay your money, take your chance. You can win the sweepstakes. This must be your lucky day. Your life is charmed. Come on, baby, Daddy needs a new pair of shoes.

As I said, fish or cut bait. If your luck be good, who needs God? If God be with ye, who needs luck?

# Honk If You Love Jesus

I n our cat-loving family, lap dogs have a bad rep. Now, a
Pekingese is your classic lap dog, a yipping, wiglike little creature that looks like something our cat might have yakked up
in one of his fits. In our family, such dogs are affectionately
referred to as "blender dogs," for reasons better left unexplained.

While idling at a traffic light one day, having nothing better to do,
we scanned the tail ends of the cars before us, always questing for
the better bumper sticker. Thank you, Paul ("The Rest of the Story")
Harvey, for making bumper-sticker hunting a national sport. On the
trim little Mazda in front of us we saw a sticker that said "I ♥ My
Pekingese."

An irony struck our teenager, who pointed and said, "Look—'I
*heart* my Pekingese'!" We understood his jest. Much as we dislike
blender dogs, we are even more irritated by those little heart symbols
we see everywhere, substituting for *love.*

The craze took off years ago in the Big Apple with a famous ad campaign: "I ♥ New York." Now everyone has joined in a kind of national confessional on wheels.

I ♥ Wisconsin.

I ♥ My Grandchildren.

I ♥ Real Butter.

Wearing one's heart on one's bumper says odd things about one's love, it seems to me. Love is flattened into a sentiment, expressed in code and stuck on a long way from the heart that feels it. These store-bought stick-on testimonials add emotional exhaust to the carbon monoxide we leave in our wakes. With exposure to sun, rain and the gravel of time, they will be reduced in the end to unreadable patches of stickum. So much for sentimentality.

Fortunately, bumper stickers laugh at their own tackiness. One bumper sticker jokes, "I Hate Bumper Stickers!" Beyond such obvious barbs one spots gentler forms of self-deprecation.

I'm Pedaling As Fast As I Can.

My Other Car Is A Porsche.

Don't Laugh. It's Paid For.

They seem to say that the clattering pickups and sputtering runabouts deserve the stickers that spot them. My favorite is the loud wail, "I'm Stuck With This THING!" It makes the rustbucket appear to be pasted on the sticker, not the other way around.

Such messages have a subtext: all this starting and stopping, the endless expense, the whole frenetic highway culture, in fact, is quite laughable and beneath our dignity—but there is no alternative. So play the game.

I Owe, I Owe, It's Off To Work I Go.

But bumper stickers point to more than the tackiness of our commuter lifestyles. They smile at worn-out values, confining gender roles, little vanities or obsessions with the trivial.

A Woman's Place Is In The Mall.

Shop Till You Drop.

Caution: This Vehicle Stops At All Garage Sales.

The preachiness of some bumper stickers is swatted around among others until the moralism of the first is undercut. Watch what happens as the slightly chiding "I Brake For Small Animals" becomes the more acid

I Brake For Small Children

then becomes the ludicrous

I Brake For Insects

then the silly

I Brake For Teddy Bears

or the mocking

I Brake For Yugos

and, finally, the mean

I Brake For Tailgaters.

This way, bumper stickers fight petty moralism with petty irony. The result is a lot of pettiness, served with a smile.

It was not always so. Try to imagine a bumper sticker on the rear end of an Assyrian war chariot, an oxcart, a stagecoach or a Conestoga wagon, ancestors of the Ford Aerostar. Why were bumper stickers then unthinkable, and why are they now not only unthinkable but ever-present?

Perhaps since "olden" days the meaning of driving has changed, and so has the significance of a vehicle. We used to ride *on* our vehicles, across a difficult terrain. Our needs were focused: get to market, slay the enemy, California or bust.

Now with our farm-sized parking lots and level superhighways we have subdued the earth. We ride *in* our vehicles. We slide in, cozy down into a temperature-controlled environment with stereophonic sound and watch pictures of the world flash by through windows shaped suspiciously like TV screens. Our needs are met in transit, not at the end of the line. We're captive in our own comforts and feel a tad bored.

A large billboard posted near Des Moines, Iowa, gave away the secret behind all this. On behalf of a local radio station it announced: "To you it's a traffic jam. To us it's a market." So it is with bumper stickers. Now that we are sealed snugly within our comforts, we are no longer travelers. We are browsers.

We do not use bumper stickers only because we want to. We use them partly because someone else understood that the driver behind us is a captive audience. Someone wants to make money by selling us words to voice our cares. The user of the bumper sticker is the advertiser's market, and the driver behind the user is the user's market.

What is for sale in that marketplace? Not only products but also allegiances to many groups and causes:

Sky Diving: You'll Fall For It.

Give Blood—Play Rugby.

Visualize World Peace.

Question Authority.

Everybody is trying to sell stock on a great big Wall Street on wheels.

From that perspective, I wince when I see a Christian witness made with traffic-jam humor:

In Case Of Rapture, This Vehicle Will Be Evacuated.

Honk If You Love Jesus.

The Christian gospel loses its poignancy when it joins the wholesale market, competing with trinkets for schlock effect. It invites cynicism. So I laugh in sympathy when I read the bumper sticker that says "Honk If You Love Bingo." Some Christians had it coming. Those who keep angling for converts with stick-on sentiments are not likely to land a miraculous draft of souls. They are more likely to get a "bumper" crop in the cheap sense of the phrase.

I ♥ Jesus.

I ♥ My Cat.

Has the Great Commission come to this?

# Yours in Christ

D earest Notes and Letters:
I apologize, as usual, for sending my monthly pep talk in photocopied form, but you'll understand, I hope, and forgive. It is impossible for me to keep up a personal correspondence with so many. From my heart, however, I send most affectionate greetings to you all, from the briefest thank-you notes among you to the most long-winded epistle, and I welcome your personal replies.

My "Inside Address" for this month can be summed up in one short sentence: "Oh, be careful, Little Letter, how you close." Your complimentary closing ought to be a parting hug or handshake, perfectly fitted to all you've said before, and an honor to the signature immediately below it.

Alas, that ideal can be elusive. It's not easy to choose between "Truly yours" and "Yours truly." "Yours," alone, can sound too clipped. "Love" is out if the correspondent doesn't really love the addressee. "Affectionately" can make the writer sound as if he or she is coming on. "Cordially" means from the heart, doesn't it? But that's not always where the writer is coming from. How about something ethnic, like "Het beste"? Or "Shalom." Or does that last one sound too Hebraic? "Peace"—or is that too sixtiesish? How about "Cheers"? Gee, that can make the writer sound British or like someone who's been drinking or watching too much TV. But "Respectfully yours" may sound too stiff. You could settle for "Sincerely" . . . but everybody says that. It sounds so insincere!

What should you do in a quandary like this? My counsel would be this. First, don't try to put your meaning into the closing words. By themselves they mean zip, nada. They're conventions, you see, conventions more worn than the rubber knob on a crutch. Saying "Sincerely" doesn't mean you're sincere. It means you've chosen the "Sincerely" convention, to the exclusion of others. Your choice may communicate nothing more than lack of hostility. It may sound merely correct or possibly warm. But it may also twang like an untuned string. Second, therefore, let the full meaning of your closing reside in your body. A pleasant closing will never disguise an unpleasant message.

To show you what I mean, let me use an extreme case. This is my real message for the month. Consider the closing "Yours in Christ." Holy-toned, is it not? And so it should be. Now imagine somewhere in the Midwest a young family, scraping along on a miserable teacher's salary. Imagine the gas bills soaring as winter winds whistle through their large but poorly insulated duplex. Downstairs, with three others, lives the owner, a young and thoughtful man, who keeps rent low and plugs holes against the cold. Then one day, in early winter, he sells the duplex back to his father and moves away. Now troubles begin.

The father, from his sprawling house in Chicago, raises rents for everyone, calling his son "weak-spined." The other young men downstairs move out, and no one else will move in. Now the small family upstairs faces $300-$400 utility costs each month. The young wife is angry, upset and broke. She writes the new owner: "How can you raise the rents at a time like this? Why do you not find new tenants for the basement? Would you at least insulate the basement so that it meets city regulations and lowers our costs? Have you no heart?" She sends evidence that the house has failed an energy audit.

He writes back: "I am entirely within my rights . . . the insulation is fine . . . you are responsible for all the utilities . . . perhaps you should seek counseling for your hysteria . . . you owe me an extra hundred dollars for snowplowing for the empty half of the duplex . . . if you move out before your contract is up, you will owe me the remainder of the year's rent . . . we will be upholding you in our prayers."

Now this man, while he lived, was a big gruff man, once a missionary, then a professor and then the president of a Christian college. Because of his patronizing manner and sanctimonious language he left a snail-trail of ill-feeling wherever he went. He was a career man of God, but even more a man of business, driving a new, white Lincoln Continental and making deals that flew. As a missionary, he had paid his dues for the Lord; the rest of his life would be Payback Time.

Now, my dear letters, imagine the effect upon our young couple when this High Priest's slippery letter closed with the words "Yours in Christ." Those poor bruised words fairly spun on the page! His signature beneath them burned to a cinder and leaked sulfurous fumes. After that, his name could not be spoken; he became known to them, long after they had moved away, as "That Devil."

Oh, be careful, Little Letters, how you close!

And I will end without closing—I wouldn't dare close, after all I've said. Instead, I leave you with these practical guidelines for the use of "Yours in Christ."

DON'T use "Yours in Christ" if you are speaking for a butthead, a scoundrel, a parasite, a jerk, a conniver, a Pharisee, a money-grubber, a tyrant, a backslapper, a fund raiser, a lender, an absentee landlord, a gossip, a rumormonger, a bird of prey, a closet perfectionist, a hit man, a backbiter, a cud chewer, a party animal, a social climber, a control freak, a contemptuous snob, a simperer, a child-abuser, a woman-hater, a critic, a bore, a weenie, a Johnny-come-lately, a collection agent, a cultural lion, a socialite, an avenger, a limousine liberal, a parrot, a nitpicker, a name-caller, a labeler, a phrasemaker, a paranoid, a publicity hound, a pollster, a politician, a solicitor, a rival, a mass mailer or a maker of lists. If you do, the words will turn on you.

FEEL FREE to close with "Yours in Christ" if you are speaking for an editor, a committee person, a rep, a secretary, a pastor, an evangelist, a superintendent or a reputable college president. But be aware, the words will have limited impact. Your reader will assume your position is doing the talking.

I RECOMMEND "Yours in Christ" for contributors, soothers, upholders, givers, "prayer warriors," confiders, nurses, elders and deacons, animal-lovers, givers of thanks, parents, teachers, "Secret Pals," visionaries, feeders of the poor, orphans, widows, suffering servants and brokenhearted ones. Their closing will be read without wincing.

# In God
# We Trust

A re pennies still money? I'm not sure. I saw one in a puddle the other day and couldn't bring myself to pick it up. So now we're letting sleeping pennies lie?

Something has changed. But what? A penny is still worth one one-hundredth of a dollar. It's still worth what it always was in proportion to other coins. It's not as though the penny had fallen on the scale. Apparently we have shifted up the scale. We've changed our concept of what's usable, what we believe in and want. Now pennies fall below our lowest rung of care.

I don't think they're money anymore.

I asked a cashier at the supermarket why he thought we still have pennies.

"I'm not sure," he said, "but I do know that if we got rid of them our sales tax would suddenly shoot up."

I hadn't thought of that. But he must have been right. We'd have to round up to the nearest nickel. We'd be staggered by it. Maybe retail sales would fall off and an already sputtering economy would fall into a fiery tailspin.

Then I got to wondering about the phrase "In God We Trust" on every penny. Is that still an idea? Or have we shifted upward on the civil-religion scale, too, and left our most familiar religious sentiment too far below the lowest rung for us to bend and pick it up?

*In. God. We. Trust.* What do those words mean? Honest Abe's been wearing them like a rain hat for years and years, but if you look close you'll see that even he's not paying attention anymore. He's staring off to the right with his lips pursed. Seems to know how silly he looks with those words on his head. Maybe he's worrying about his hairdo. He must know his rain hat is full of holes.

Take *God.* In recent Gallup polls, more than 86 percent of all Americans considered themselves Christian, but less than half knew who preached the Sermon on the Mount. Sixty percent of the country was in church last Easter, but one out of four people there didn't know what Easter celebrates. God has been looking increasingly like a DWM (dead white male), so he's been feminized, ethnicized and personalized—when he's not been ostracized.

With the New Age movement, God has become especially easy to find: just look in a mirror. One of the early Westernizers of Eastern mysticism, Alan Watts, said in 1959 after taking an experimental dose of LSD: "You yourself are the eternal energy of the universe playing hide-and-go seek . . . with itself. At root you are the Godhead, for God is all there is." If there ever was an idea people are inclined to accept, there it is.

Now you're a god. I'm a god. Everywhere a god god . . . Old MacDonald was a god. E-I-E-I-O.

And *we?* Who is that? Once we thought we lived in a melting pot. Now we know we're in a salad bowl. Used to be that black was divided from white. Now both black and white are divided from poor black and poor white. Black youths are divided from Korean grocers and Hasidic Jews. Black gangs from Hispanic and Cambodian and Puerto Rican gangs. Everybody from Native Americans. We have providers and parasites, the insured and the unsure, spin doctors and media junkies. Homies, homeless, homos and ho's. And every gun defended by the NRA whispers "Not *we* but *me.*"

We're in a mess. Our schools are integrated but our minds are not. And *trust?* What is that? Your check is no good at McDonald's. To validate your purchase you will need your social-security number and two picture IDs. Everybody owns your face. And accidents hardly ever happen anymore, only negligent and malicious acts, ripe for litigation. The words over Abe's head ought to read "See You in Court."

In general, we've slid from "In God We Trust" to "What We Trust In (Michael Jordan, Bud Lite, experts, MTV, etc.) Is God." Trust is the empty space we move in when our myths have failed. Myths like Magic Johnson. And because we have arrived at a sense of trust that entails no commitment, these words on our coins may stay. We've legally removed practically every other public sign of overlap between the interests of church and state. Presumably, if these words were a threat of any kind, they would have been removed, too.

"In God We Trust."

I don't think it's an idea any more. But when I recall what the cashier said, I begin to wonder what tax would take a leap if we gave it up.

# God Bless America

*I* 've heard people argue that "God Bless America," the Kate Smith rendition to be exact, should be our national anthem.

I've heard construction workers mutter "God bless America" when a leggy young woman walked by.

I've heard a card player say "God bless America" when another player passed gas.

We've all heard presidential candidates end rousing stump speeches with the words "God bless America."

I'm confused. Is "God bless America" one phrase or four?

# God

S omebody named Deidre Sullivan recently did a national survey and published the results in a book called *What Do We
Mean When We Say God?* Maybe you read about it in the
newspapers. Sullivan asked about seven hundred people from
different professions and religious backgrounds what the word *God*
brings to mind.

Some answers were fuzzier than a mohair sweater, like this one:
"God is a kind word, a helping hand, forgiveness." Not so fuzzy was
the one from a Berkeley lawyer, who said that sometimes when she
meditates, "God comes up as my grandmother with a frying pan in
her hand." (She didn't say whether the frying pan was for frying or
for banging someone on the head.) One man pictures God as a train
rushing past a grasshopper on a milkweed pod.

From the Reverend Daniel Martin, a priest in Rye, New York, came
one of the more interesting responses. Glancing back toward the
ancient Germanic root *gudam,* which meant "called" or "invoked,"

Rev. Martin suggests that *God* means " 'one who is greeted.' God is the mystery of life we greet. . . . The mystery is in everything. When we recognize it and try to put a word on it, it's 'Hey!' "

That's fresh.

Unfortunately, these answers are not truly representative of what people mean when they say "God." Sullivan surveyed professionals—thinking people—about how they use the word when they use it thinkingly. Those seven hundred were asked to use the word *God* in a discourse about the nature of divinity. Naturally, under those circumstances one would impart some meaning to it. But the 249,999,301 or so Americans she did not interview are more likely to say the word *God* without a glimmer of reflection.

People are saying "God" thoughtlessly, right now, all over the world, wherever English is spoken. In courtrooms, witnesses are being sworn in with "Do you swear to tell the truth, the whole truth and nothing but the truth, so help you God?" Tough guys are vowing revenge, saying, "So help me God, I'm going to kill that sucker." People ogling the yachts in the harbor are saying, "God, I wish I had one of those." Others banging their thumbs with upholstery hammers are finding other creative uses for the name. And teenage girls, at least the ones in my neighborhood, are saying "Omigod" to express any of the following: (1) "Wow," (2) "No kidding," (3) "Oh no," (4) "Oh boy," (5) "What on earth?" or even (6) "Hello."

*God* must be about the most-often-used word in the English language, second only to the word *I.*

You'd think it would have some meaning. But its ordinary function, in our times, is to serve as an exclamation or vow, trading up a few of its ancient associations with power, justice, love and eternity to intensify whatever else the speaker is saying. It's an oral equivalent of underlining. Or, to picture it another way, using *God* in conversational vows is like pitching a rock into the ocean to emphasize a point. The effect can be dramatic, thanks to the difference in size between the boundless ocean and the arrogant little thrower. But the meaning of the gesture is in the throwing. No one asks where the rock lands. No one confuses the throw with the study of oceanography. One is content to let the rock vanish into the vasty deep.

So degraded is the word in ordinary parlance, so dead, that it stirs a longing in me for a verbal resurrection. What if I stood on the midnight shore, slinging my rocks—"Hey!" "Hey!" "Hey!" And in the crashing of the waves, again and again, I heard the ocean reply, "Yahweh," "Yahweh," "Yahweh"? What if I stood at the rim of the Grand Canyon, shouting "Yoohoo!" and the echo came back: "Who, you?" I think I would be moved. And then, remembering the Hebrew's unpronounceable tetragrammaton, YHWH, the sacred name, I would suggest to everyone I knew that the same be done with *God.* Spell it G * D. Or call it the "G-word." Take it out of circulation. Maybe its value would increase.

# Godsend

S ome time ago the population of Santa Barbara, California, passed a course you might call "Godsend 101." First came a horrendous landscape fire—a short course in hell that was later reported round the world, as the spark from a short-circuit in an arsonist's brain spread in a racing Great Wall of flame. It blackened citrus groves, turned oily eucalyptus trees into bombs, vaulted a six-lane divided highway and reamed out hundreds of homes, some worth millions, leaving little amid the charcoal but tiled swimming pools and Porsche bodies resting on rubberless rims. No one said it was an "act of God." Whatever feelings of terror, awe and anger blasted through the public mind, all were conspicuously tempered by shame. Everyone knew this was a "mansend."

Then came water. Days and weeks of spring rain, which, after five years' drought, the earth sucked in through cracked lips and gaping jaws. After a joyful week of rain, what the earth could not swallow ran down its chin. Gibraltar Reservoir—full! Lake Cachuma—up from

16 percent to more than 40 percent of capacity. Now pleasure boats and dangling docks had something to float about. Santa Barbara, long gullivered by water politics and growing used to air-injected low-flow toilets that take off like jet bombers, now had a two-year lease on life. The TV and newspaper people referred to the deluge as the "March Miracle." But even the sybarites of Santa Barbara, noted for their spirituality more than their faith, found justification for using the word "godsend."

Even if the word, with a small *g*, meant little more than "Gee, we were incredibly lucky this time," it still reflected well on big *G*. The way they said it was the opposite of swearing. They saved it for a time when the heavens, through five years of closed-fistedness, had amply demonstrated the folly of human managerial posturing. They said it looking up, not at the magnitude of human malfeasance but at the possibility of divine munificence. They said it, as I heard it in the grocery stores, with a sense of appreciation for blessings bestowed, willing to credit their "miracle" to the highest reach in the firmament. They said it almost in the spirit of Psalm 68:9-10: "You gave abundant showers, O God. . . . Your people settled in it, and from your bounty, O God, you provided for the poor."

So the Santa Barbarians, as some jokingly refer to themselves, passed Godsend 101, and I with them. But what if this were a school? What would we study in our sophomore year? What courses would I take if I wanted to major in Godsend? What would I learn in my Senior Seminar?

The only way to find out, I guess, is to flip through the course catalog, then maybe talk to my Adviser. Darn committee prose. I can hardly tell what's on the syllabi. Well, here's the sequence for Godsend majors. Looks like quite a few electives:

□ *Godsend 102, "Advanced Freshman Godsend."* A continuation of Godsend 101, involving further identification and appreciation of miraculously timed positive interventions in the lives of individuals and communities. Required texts: Genesis 41, *Pharaoh's Dream: The Fat and the Lean;* also Luke 12:13-34, *The Parable of the Rich Fool.*

☐ *Business 214, "A Success Ethic for the Nineties."* Discussions of the popular themes "Looking Out for #1," "God Wants You to Succeed" and "You've Got It Coming." One short paper required. No tests. Required text: Psalm 118:25, "O LORD, save us; O LORD, grant us success."

☐ *Communications 206, "And Now from Our Sponsor."* An examination of the rhetoric of promise and delivery in modern televangelism; special focus on deconstructive analyses of marketing appeals for Christian prayer bricks, dog tags, bookends and pocket charms. Required text: Acts 8:9-25, *Simon the Sorcerer.*

☐ *Meteorology 214, "With Precipitation for All."* A statistical survey of patterns of precipitation, by historical epoch and geographical region, in relation to normative understandings of justice. Required text: Matthew 5—6, *The Sermon on the Mount;* recommended text: Matthew 5:45, "He causes his sun to rise on the evil and the good, and sends rain on the righteous and the unrighteous."

☐ *Philosophy 210, "Intermediate Epistemology."* A Socratic-style symposium on ways of knowing "what's happening" preceded by semantic investigation of the terms *fate, fortune, luck* and *providence.* Required text: Job 38:35, "Do you send the lightning bolts on their way? Do they report to you, 'Here we are'?"

☐ *Psychology 324, "The Psychopathology of Belief."* Mostly lecture and weekly experimental labs, seeking to define behavioral, psychoneurological and genetic factors in erroneous thinking. Required text: 2 Thessalonians 2:11, "For this reason God sends them a powerful delusion . . ." Recommended for pre-law students.

☐ *Theology 310, "Introduction to Eschatology: You Thought You Had a Bad Day."* An inquiry into "the last things." Lecture only. Recommended text: Ezekiel 14:21, "How much worse will it be when I send against Jerusalem my four dreadful judgments—sword and famine and wild beasts and plague—to kill its men and their animals!"

☐ *Theology 311, "Intermediate Eschatology: By Appointment Only."* A continuation of 310. Lecture only. An inquiry into the structure of divine mediation. Required text: Acts 3:19-20, "Repent, then, . . . that he may send the Christ, who has been appointed for you."

☐ *Theology 312, "Advanced Eschatology: Election Day."* A continuation of 311. Lecture only. Theme: "Unlocking the mysteries of election." Required text: Mark 13:27, "And he will send his angels and gather his elect from the four winds."

☐ *Theology 401, "The Cost of Discipleship."* Lecture, discussion and field work concerning radical evangelical interpretations of *Godsend.* Required texts: John 20:21, "As the Father has sent me, I am sending you"; Matthew 10:16, "I am sending you out like sheep among wolves. Therefore be as shrewd as snakes and as innocent as doves."

☐ *Senior Honors Project, Independent Study.* Major lifelong project required in consultation with Adviser.

# Act of God

*I*n legal parlance, an "act of God" is an unforeseeable or inevitable occurrence, such as a tornado, caused by nature and not by human beings.

In a recent morning newspaper, the phrase took on a cloudier meaning. Highway 101, the sole direct artery linking Los Angeles with coastal cities to the north, was reported blocked at Seacliff, north of Ventura, when a Southern Pacific freight train derailed, dumping seventy-six drums of aqueous hydrazine, a suspected carcinogen. Eight drums broke, their dangerous fumes driving more than three hundred people from their homes and forcing thousands of testy motorists on a thirty-five-mile detour through winding mountain roads.

The cause of the derailment was not in dispute, but the cause of the cause was. It was agreed that a bearing had overheated, causing an axle to snap off a car. A Federal Railroad Administration official called the overheating "a freak thing, one of those acts of God." She insisted: "It's like something we call 'summer kinks,' when a track heats up and melts and causes an accident. It's just an act of God."

A state safety official disagreed. "It could be a bearing, but then again it could be a faulty axle," he said. "It's premature to call this an act of God. I haven't heard anything from my staff that answers the question [of cause]."

These people standing around arguing whether God was to blame were not theologians. They were railroad types. No indication that they were in a worshiping mood. To public officials like these, the phrase "act of God" appears to mean anything from "I haven't got a clue" to "Don't look at me." Comedian Flip Wilson used to bag a lot of laughs with the line "The devil made me do it!" but the officials who blame God are serious, even though they are copping out in basically the same way. God, for them, is the darkness just beyond our little patch of light.

Our race prides itself on control: we dam up rivers, seed clouds, bomb volcanoes, tow icebergs, harness wind, waves and sunshine, tread the moon. But when somebody gets hurt, it's an act of God. When a tornado flattens a mobile-home park, God did it. We forget who passed zoning laws that allow a mobile home to sit on a few cinder blocks tethered by a rusty chain.

Fires race down mountainsides, charring million-dollar homes. Act of God. But who failed to clear the underbrush? Who put up wood shake roofs that could be lit with a sparkler? Who built those tinder-boxes on desert slopes where fires have raged for eons, part of the ecological cycle?

In tragic Bangladesh, cows, dogs, carts and thousands of human bodies lie lodged in mud as flood waters recede. Act of God, we say, but we forget that a natural flood plain had been sucked dry by "civilized" water projects upriver. The flood plain become a death-trap when the overgrazing of a watershed made dams burst.

How many so-called "acts of God" are really acts or inactions of our own? Countless, to be sure. But how many other events in our world—besides the miraculous healings, the prophetic visions, the answered prayers—might better deserve to be called acts of God?

A feathered one, outside my window, chirps on the night-blooming cereus.

One speaks encouragingly to an obese child.

There is one in a marriage bed, where pride melts beneath forgiveness.

One is running for office, without corruption.

One yields the right of way.

One simply thickens the gravy.

# Good Thoughts

*L*ovely Avelina had wide curling lips and black-rimmed glasses that shadowed her Mexican ash-brown cheeks. All summer long, at an academic institute, she had carried the secret of her pregnancy behind her sweet smile. Now, in a fireside room by the ocean on our last day, as we read parting appreciations to our colleagues and newfound friends, Avelina was not among us. Word came that she was in the hospital.

Quickly everyone read the signs: she had visited her doctor the day before. Some of us knew that. Today she was having surgery. The surgeon, we were informed, was an obstetrician. All around the fireplace, we rustled with anxiety: she must be having a D & C. She must be losing her baby!

I was in a church service once when an older man, overweight and sloppily dressed, sitting inconspicuously in the back pew, suddenly arched his back and yelled "Uhhhh!" as if he had been shot with an arrow. As he went purple and slid to the floor, a nurse and several others rushed to attend him. We all stirred, assuming, I guess, that he was having a heart attack or a stroke or a serious convulsion and might not be long for this world.

The minister, to his credit, never broke stride. He bowed his head with one hand on his forehead and stretched the other hand out over the congregation, poised like a surfer. "Let's pray right now," he said, "that God will show mercy to our brother. Father, if it is your will, restore this stricken brother to health and spare him from the hand of lasting harm . . ." He went on, expertly riding the emotion as if it were a wave. When he was through, everyone felt calm, uplifted, more unified and collectively closer to God. When news came back about fifteen minutes later that what the man had suffered was merely an intense back spasm that had left him sore but undamaged, it was received lovingly and with good humor.

Something similar, but significantly different, happened in our room by the ocean. As we shared gasps and anguished glances over Avelina's probable loss, a woman from Bolivia said words that rescued everyone from fear: "We should not assume the worst. Let's all just think good thoughts for Avelina."

"Yes," everyone echoed. "That's right."

Think good thoughts for Avelina.

The effect of these words was immediate. Our frowns turned to concerned smiles. In a group with no particular religion, a mixture of Protestants, Catholics, Jews, agnostics and spiritualists of various stripes, this summons to think good thoughts conveyed an acceptable form of wisdom, calmed fluttering hearts, uplifted our vision and forged a social unity deeper than we had felt before. It was about as great an infusion of spirituality into our proceedings as a professional gathering under the sponsorship of the state of California could allow. It was almost like prayer.

So much like prayer, in fact, that I for one began to ask myself, "Is that what this is?" While Avelina's health and that of her unborn child were foremost in our minds, there was no good time to engage in intellectual speculation about doctrines or words or shades of spirituality, and yet I was forced to reflect by an emptiness I felt at the base of my skull. The Bolivian woman's gesture had been timely and bold. I respected it. Her words had been soothing and caring. I appreciated them. But I could not shake the impression that in such a gathering a call to "think good thoughts" was a pale civic parody of a summons to prayer.

Why think good thoughts? What would they do, except provide private soothings for us? At that very moment Avelina might have been having her baby extracted from her, unborn. Could good thoughts save her baby? Could they heal Avelina?

During the mid-eighties, back when crystals were in vogue, I read an article about crystals. It claimed that when the mind thinks, it subtly alters all relationships in the space-time continuum. Most people don't realize the power at their disposal, but that power is infinite. It can be harnessed to bring us rewards if we know how to focus our mental emanations with crystal "power wands" and other paraphernalia. Obviously, the New Age hardware salespeople had faith in the power of "good thoughts." Taken to the extreme, they could disclose the godhood within us.

I thought at the time that the "crystal power" fad was a trick on the feeble-minded, but I have since uncovered some of its deeper, less flaky roots in Eastern philosophy. For example, in *Fourteen Lessons in Yogi Philosophy* by Yogi Ramacharaka, novices are taught that "Thoughts are Things"—that thoughts can be seen as cloudlike apparitions with one's psychic vision. Moreover, thoughts attract similar thoughts to themselves and so gather force. All things, says the yogi, are charged with "Prana," a portion of the all-pervading vital force. "The man of strong will sending forth a vigorous positive thought," says the yogi,

> sends with it a supply of Prana proportioned to the force with which the thought was propelled. Such thoughts are often sent like a bullet to the mark, instead of drifting along slowly like an ordinary thought emanation. . . . Those high in occult development frequently send thought-forms to aid and help their fellow-

beings when in distress or need, and many of us have experienced the effect of helpful thoughts sent in this manner.

I don't know whether anyone in our room by the ocean was committed to yogic philosophy, but I know that terms and concepts imported from it—auras, mantras, meditation, clairvoyance, telepathy, human magnetism, mental healing, astral projection, spiritual planes, chakras, spirit guides, karma, reincarnation and so on—fill our boutiques and our magazines and our popular speech. We in the West have grown quite comfortable with them, enough so that we sometimes do not even mark their presence. But when we were told just to "think good thoughts for Avelina," I detected their presence. It was as if I had stumbled across a tiny cracked shell from the East washed up on the beach.

The Eastern philosophies that have spawned so many of our Western pop-psych trinkets are thought-systems of exquisite beauty, and yet I find even greater beauty in truth. When I was asked to "think good thoughts for Avelina," I think it was the absence of a truth that made me feel the emptiness at the base of my skull. I had no confidence at all that our good thoughts had power to oppose the great enemy of babies. Yet none of the Christians in our oceanside room offered to pray aloud that day. None including me. For all I know, the Maker of Avelina and her baby has never yet heard from us our cry for help.

I know only one way to restore myself to the beauty of that higher truth. Only one way to fill the emptiness in the midst of my "good thoughts." And that is to say,

Lord, spare Avelina, if that is pleasing to you,
and spare her unborn child,
and draw us all into closer accordance
with your whole and perfect will.

# God Never Sends Us Burdens Greater Than We Can Bear

F ive years have passed since the funeral, and only now are my wife and I starting to be able to talk about it. We've turned down invitations to some of our best friends' homes because we know the conversation will swing around to Dougie. Sarah stopped going to her coffee ministry, and she hired a different baby sitter because the old one had a way of saying things. Like she came up from under the couch once with a squeeze dinosaur and said, "These teeth marks must be Dougie's. Don't you miss him?" Even though she meant well, she was totally insensitive to our pain. I think she feared it.

Of course, meaning well and speaking well aren't the same thing. That's what we found out. And I'm not even sure that everybody means as well as they let on, if you get right down to the bottom of it. I mean, here we are standing in the receiving line. Sarah's in a chair because her legs won't hold her, and I'm standing, but my legs are made of water. We're ten feet away from the coffin, but the smells of gardenias and gladioli and daffodils and whatnot are swirling around our heads so thick we can hardly breathe. In a way, it's a glorious moment because you've cried your tears and made some kind of horrible peace with God and now you're standing there talking to people, even smiling at the parents of your little boy's friends, and hugging your own family like you're holding each other up. People tell you that you've been a comfort to them, as if they were the ones having a hard time looking at their little boy's face in that coffin. It's sort of glorious because you're living with a strange, glowing intensity like you've never felt before. All the loops on the carpet stand out, and you're probably the only one hearing the faint clicks of the light bulbs in the floor lamps. You're a kind of Superman. But it's horrible, because it's not really you. You're out of your body somewhere, watching this whole thing go on. And even though you've made your peace with God and said all the prayers, you haven't really made peace. Your heart is off somewhere battling with God, just pounding on his chest.

I kept thinking of barbecue. As I was meeting people in the line, I kept saying to myself, *You're barbecued.* I couldn't stop thinking it. It made me crazy.

Sarah took it a little different from me. She cried so much more, but crying didn't seem to wash anything out of her. She had to hang onto someone all the time. She was barbecued, too. I could see it, even though with all the busyness we hardly found time to talk, except when the minister was over.

And then this lady comes through the line. She hardly knows us. And she didn't know Dougie at all, I'm sure. And the first thing she says is, "He has such a sweet smile." *Yes,* I'm thinking, *and that sweet smile cost him his life.* It's an unbearable thought. Here he goes in, he goes in for routine oral surgery to correct an underbite, he's in for over an hour, everything's fine, and they give him his brand-new smile, and he never comes out of the anesthetic. He never comes out of it. Never. So I just about cave in when she says that about his smile. And I squash her hands and close my eyes and drop my head for a second and she hugs me and pats me on the back and whispers in my ear, "Hang in there. God never sends us burdens greater than we can bear." I nod my head yes without looking up and pass her along to my wife. But inside I'm screaming—I can hardly shake the next person's hand—I'm screaming, *What do you know? What do you know?*

Five years after the funeral, I've started to emerge from what feels like a long hibernation. We've had another child. We remodeled our kitchen. We, Sarah and I, went through a long time where we couldn't touch each other, and we'd start up these little arguments over nothing, a chance phrase, and then we wouldn't let the argument go on. We'd just crush it with this ten-ton iron weight. But we've had counseling and read books and gone on some kind of hard vacations, and gradually maybe surprised each other with a stroke on the arm or a telephone call in the middle of the day between our places of work. And we've had some laughs lately, played a few games. I'm starting to function, and Sarah has gone from one real friend to two and lately to a group of about six who keep seeing each other. They play racquetball. And every weekday afternoon at 4:30 she ties on her Reeboks and runs for miles along the gravel roads. All by herself. She's a good runner, it turns out, but she pushes herself until she feels like she has to vomit.

So with all the new voices in our lives, and the new baby, and people starting to feel it's safe to approach us once again, after five years of slow, convulsive healing, what do you think sticks in my mind? It's that phrase: "God never gives us burdens greater than we can bear."

What a crock. What a stab in my inner ear at the very moment when I needed total love, total understanding, total healing. It was a placebo. I'm sure she felt good about what she said. Maybe somebody said it to her once and she thought it was original. It was funeral talk. Christian. It sounded optimistic. But most of all, it allowed her to get past me in that line without having to feel anything like what I felt. It was empty, empty consolation.

Must I congratulate God for the wise decision to snatch away this little boy with the jutting jaw before he could even once see his new face in the mirror? Was it the hand of God that reached out from the deadly gas and pinched off his brain waves? Whatever happened to the Angel of Death? The Lord of the Flies? How could I believe in a God who holds me up with one hand and, for his pleasure, smashes me flat with the other? And what, pray tell, *would* be a burden greater than I could bear? What would be the look of a man who could not bear it anymore? Are there no runaways, no cracked brains, no suicides in this world? No cynics? No God-haters? Would I have to physically explode to disprove the lady's caramel-coated little point?

I will say it: I do not think that the death of my son was a present from God, and I do not think that I bore it. My wife can speak for herself, but I felt a desolation within my soul for so long, a desolation that awed the ministers who tried to comfort me. They had no deeper experience than mine to offer up, only thoughts, which are no adequate substitute for knowledge such as I was granted. I believe that I was teaching my comforters the nature of pain, the infinity of red darkness in the human soul. It was a complete and honest emptiness, and to this day I have it in me. I always had, but I never knew it. Now I have found it and built a safety wall around it and placed a decorative roof over it, planted flowers all around it and laid merry flagstones leading to it. But when I go there with my bucket, I throw a stone in. The stone disappears from view and I hear no splash. Nothing. No echo. No reverberation. It is the most silent silence I can imagine. And I walk away with my bucket unfilled.

I could not bear that discovery. But I did get through it. How? I thought again and again of Christ with nails through his ankles and palms. There he was, father and son in one package, rejected by everyone and dying of thirst and loss of blood. He could not bear it either. He died of it. I told myself over and over: *nothing you have experienced, in all of your pain, is greater than that.* And yet at the point where I give up and am ready to throw myself in the bottomless well, he bears it. He grabs the nails that pin him to the wood. He

embraces his captors in his outstretched arms. He says, I go into the
devil's own territory for you. And I come back, with a new body.
Come, let me hold you.

You cannot bear it.

But I can bear *you*.

# R.I.P.

W yatt Earp. Bat Masterson. Dodge City. Boot Hill.
Tombstones jutting, flat, skewed, a bad tooth gray.
Cashiered cowboys. NO SALE.
　　What was it ripped? Flesh from soul?
　　Miss Kitty's heart? The temple veil?

Rest in peace, oh spirit prone to fly.
We wore black to fool you, made candelabra flicker,
crawled a winding road to and from the bones.
Lost you good.

Stay there now, boxed in pine.
We hammered more than necessary
nails. Six feet of Kansas clay should hold,
and stones for weight. Lots of little stones
and last the big one, chiseled pretty,

      R.I.P.
but sharp and heavy like a knee
on your twitching neck.

And if the weight of those precautions
prove too light,
let these words that speed you to the Bosom—
"May he rest in peace"—also curb
   your spirit's flight.

# Mansions in Glory

*I* n mansions of glory and endless delight,
I'll ever adore Thee in heaven so bright . . .
When I'm not thinking hard, my mental image of heaven
comes filtered through the phrase "mansions in glory." After
a lifetime's repetitions of verse four of the old hymn "My Jesus, I Love
Thee," that phrase is part of the hard-wiring of my mind. But there's
a glitch. The phrase in the hymn is "mansions *of* glory," as if those
heavenly mansions are built out of glory instead of bricks and boards.
And yet I remember it as "mansions *in* glory," a much more "home-
ly" conception. The mansion my imagination conjures for itself is a
purely physical one, a huge estate with eight-foot stone walls, coach
houses, a $300,000 security system, a manor house the size of a
hospital, a Bentley in the circular drive and swans silently unzipping
a twelve-acre pond. With a twist of the channel selector I can tune
in images of celebrity hangouts on the cliffs of Malibu, with palm-
lined drives, pink marble terraces and private screening rooms. Or

ballrooms and white-columned porches in Scarlett O'Hara's pre-Civil War South.

I can't speak confidently for others, but I suspect I'm not the only one to make that unconscious slide from *of* to *in*. Why? Perhaps because "mansions *of* glory" requires a spiritual imagination, whereas "mansions *in* glory" requires only a material, and the material imagination threatens less to change us from within.

With my material imagination, I equate heaven with *havin'*. Havin' everything we lack here on earth. Got scrawny biceps? In heaven, you'll get a body by Joe Weider. Driving a rattletrap? In heaven, you'll fly. Feeling alienated from your mate? In heaven, every second in the presence of God and the saints will be an intensity of bliss that will make sexual climax look like a Parcheesi tournament. Maybe you're feeling stressed. Not to worry. In heaven, you'll have plenty to do and all the time in the universe to do it. And you won't need money. Everything will be free. You'll have enormous appetites, and they'll be fully satisfied, with leftovers for snacks.

The material imagination of eternity didn't originate with me. It was well apparent in Jesus' eleven disciples, who were so knuckle-headed that Jesus had to use simple material imagery as a kind of can opener to gain entrance to their thoughts. When Jesus told them he was going away, referring to his crucifixion and resurrection, they didn't get it. So he reassured them by using the simple language of travel and lodging: "In my Father's house are many *monai;* if it were not so, I would have told you. I am going there to prepare a place for you. And if I go and prepare a place for you, I will come back and take you to be with me that you also may be where I am" (Jn 14:2-3). Does that sound as if Jesus is saying "Read my lips"? It sounds that way in Greek, too.

Unfortunately, the scholars who did the King James translation of the Bible threw us a slider by translating *monai* as "mansions." At the time of James I, the word *mansion* was barely beginning to take on its present connotations of "stately residence." For two hundred years previously it had meant something much closer to the sense of its French cognate, *maison,* namely, a place to stay, a dwelling or place of steady residence. The NIV gets back to the most sensible translation: "In my Father's house are many rooms."

Rooms, unlike mansions, are easy to visualize inside a house, though they come uncomfortably close to suggesting a heaven laid out like a Benedictine monastery, full of tiny cells—or worse yet, a library bordered with carrels. What a cruel joke it would be to wake up from a short sleep of death and find oneself slumped in one of those, laboring over an eternal research paper!

Elsewhere, however, the New Testament supplies imagery that helps free Jesus' figures of speech from blinkered material imaginations. The apostle Paul in his second letter to the Corinthians shakes his readers loose from a literal mentality by direct statement: "So we fix our eyes not on what is seen, but on what is unseen. For what is seen is temporary, but what is unseen is eternal" (4:18). Then, to prevent his readers from "seeing" in the temporal sense, he pitches his message about the afterlife in language rife with mixed metaphors. Without an Old Testament context, his words might seem like a bewildering hodgepodge of building imagery, tent imagery, clothing imagery and body imagery:

> Now we know that if the earthly tent we live in is destroyed, we have a building from God, an eternal house in heaven, not built by human hands. Meanwhile we groan, longing to be clothed with our heavenly dwelling, because when we are clothed, we will not be found naked. For while we are in this tent, we groan and are burdened, because we do not wish to be unclothed but to be clothed with our heavenly dwelling, so that what is mortal may be swallowed up by life. (2 Cor 5:1-4)

Try to picture a person covering up his or her nakedness with a— building? (Just a moment while I slip into something a little more architectural . . . ) It's almost laughable.

The language makes better sense against a background of the ancient Israelites' spiritual journey, which was often synonymous with their physical journey from nomadic wanderings to a Jerusalem they could call home. For the Israelites, packing up and moving their tents and folding tabernacle was an exertion of faith, often in the face of apparently insurmountable odds. It was obedience in action; thus it brought them closer to the true center of their destiny, a permanent physical and spiritual home. The writer of Hebrews, in his catalog of the heroes of faith, describes the archetype of this movement, Abraham, as having "lived in tents, as did Isaac and Jacob, who were heirs with him of the same promise. For he was looking forward to the city with foundations, whose architect and builder is God" (Heb 11:9-10). That city, in the multilayered language of the writer of Hebrews, is both Jerusalem, the capital of the Promised Land, and "the New Jerusalem," the capital of eternity, so to speak.

To speak in general terms, then, in Israel's experience the transient gave way to the permanent, which gave way to the eternal. From that abstract outline of the process leading to satisfaction of the fundamental national desire sprang the following parallel lines of concrete images:

| | | |
|---|---|---|
| tents | ⇨ houses | ⇨ mansions in glory |
| tabernacle | ⇨ temple | ⇨ no temple *(see below)* |
| desert | ⇨ Promised Land | ⇨ "New Jerusalem" |
| flesh | ⇨ spirit | ⇨ new spiritual body |
| unclothed | ⇨ clothed | ⇨ "clothed" with new life |
| natural objects | ⇨ made with hands | ⇨ made by God |

Paul could fiddle with these terms because their figurative sense was already part of the national vocabulary. But by conspicuously mixing the metaphors he was wringing new sense out of them, shearing off material references and refocusing his reference on the transcendent common denominator.

The key to the deeper meaning of this mystically tinted rhetoric may be found in an even more mystically symbolic book, The Revelation of St. John, particularly in the description of "the New Jerusalem" in the second to last chapter. There, after all the history of

Jewish striving to build and maintain a temple, it comes as quite a surprise to see John write: "I did not see a temple in the city, because the Lord God Almighty and the Lamb are its temple" (Rev 21:22). Such words are a final blow to the material imagination. The temple, and with it everything that might surround the body—tents, tabernacles, buildings, clothes, rooms—evaporates. And we are left with just the body. Even the body, conceived as a cloak of mortal flesh worn by an immortal spirit, vanishes as such and is replaced by a glorified body, so that, as Paul says, "what is mortal may be swallowed up by life."

Full, pure, all-consumed life, in other words, is the "place/not-place" where the redeemed soul travels/not-travels after death. Not some Hearst Castle in the sky, not even some material little room with an otherwordly glow about it. Personally, I find my mind defeated when I try to imagine it, except to the extent that I can extrapolate from those moments in life when a surge of spiritual joy makes experience seem to outstrip word, time, place and thing. Paul speaks of that Spirit's work as a guarantee of what is to come.

From that perspective, then, the hymn had it right. The body's mansion *in* glory is a mansion *of* glory . . . but the mansion is a place, a place of glory, and the place is the body, a glorified body, and the glory of the body is its being in the presence of God. Bein', not havin'. That, I suspect, is Life.

And what's Life?

God only knows.